OLD CHURCH
NEW CHURCH

OLD CHURCH
NEW CHURCH

A HISTORICAL PERSPECTIVE ON
HOW THE CHURCH IS CHANGING

DR. LEO BARNWELL

WinePressPublishing
Great Books, Defined.

WinePress Publishing (PO Box 428, Enumclaw, WA 98022) functions only as book publisher. As such, the ultimate design, content, editorial accuracy, and views expressed or implied in this work are those of the author.

ISBN 13: 978-1-4141-1915-1
ISBN 10: 1-4141-1915-1
Library of Congress Catalog Card Number: 2010912464

CONTENTS

ACKNOWLEDGMENTS

I FIRST GIVE honor to my mom, Dollie Bellamy, and dad, the late Elder David Barnwell, for representing Christ at church and at home, and demonstrating the value of doing right regardless of the cost. I thank Rick Joyner and the Morning Star Ministry in Charlotte, North Carolina, for their demonstration of cutting edge ideas of the new church. I want to thank the saints at New Bethel of Fayetteville, North Carolina, who are second to none for demonstrating their hunger for God. I want to thank the saints of Faith Community Church, of Lumberton, North Carolina, who are recognizing the differences between the old and the new and are moving forward in spite of fears, oppositions, and sacrifices.

Most importantly, I want to thank my wife, who is deserving of all the benefits and rewards due to her for her patience during this writing. I'm also appreciative to my children—two daughters, their husbands, my son, and his wife, who are recognizing the challenges of the church set before them and are ready to accept their responsibility in the service of the King. And lastly, to my grandchildren, who will one day read this text and hopefully better understand and be inspired to continue the important task of making a distinction in the church and a difference in the world. To all of these, I'm deeply grateful.

INTRODUCTION

IT WAS DURING the summer of 2009, a thought concerning the church being ready for the Lord's return surfaced again in my mind. I had often heard that these were the last days and Jesus is coming soon. I wondered, if Jesus is coming back soon, there's a lot that must happen in His church. There is a great gulf between how the church is and how the church should be, as the perfect bride fit for her Bridegroom.

In my meditations, I communed with the Lord:

> Lord, as I look at the condition of the church today, and the way it should be in Your return, You've got a lot of work to do in Your church....It's going to be interesting to see how You bring Your church to become who she should be.

The image I had of watching the church change was one of passively watching things unfold, like watching a movie at the theater. The Lord gently corrected me: "It's not going to happen that way. It will not happen with you passively taking a position to watch change unfold without your doing something about it. When you find out how the church should be, and begin to speak it, then I will do it."

From this point, I became confident that this change will happen with those participants who pursue change with ideas of God's unfolding plan and purpose. Those who recognize that the church is in a season of change should seek God's wisdom as revealed in historical trends as well as the biblical text. Then the church can better see her need for change, and as the bride, prepare herself for her Bridegroom.

This is a purpose of this discourse. Thoughts that provide the backdrop of the research include such questions as these:

- In the light of change happening in the world, how is the church changing?
- What ideas of the New Testament church have been lost in the church today?
- What are the ideas and practices that have historically shaped the church into who she is today?
- As change occurs, what things should remain and what should change?

As members of God's church, many believers have a passion to see a move of God in the church and the world. These moves become significant for Christ preparing His church for His return. However, these moves should also cause the church to reexamine and wrestle with important paradigms of the *old* that can either hinder or give birth to something *new*. New wine requires new wineskins, because the old cannot contain it.

My target audience for this discourse is for those in training for ministry in churches and seminaries, where persons may critically examine the condition of the church and consider the important things for moving the church forward. Second, it is for church leaders, who should address these issues because many recognize that change is happening, and leaders will better understand, evaluate, and communicate how change should also preserve important foundational truths. Also thirdly, at the risk of trying to cover too large of an audience, it is also my hope that any believer can read this text and become better familiar with the condition of the church and take some responsibility for moving it forward.

I do not consider this discourse a final word concerning how the church should be, but I intend it to encourage discussion, dialogue, and debate for moving the church into new paradigms and discovering new ways for looking at old truths.

Old Hat, New Hat

One of my grandchildren's favorite books (or my favorite) is *Old Hat, New Hat* (Stan and Jan Berenstain, New York, Random House, 1970).

Ms. Berenstain Bear went in the hat store with intentions of buying a new hat, but nothing new was good enough to replace her old hat. Each hat was either: "too big, too small, too flat, too tall; too loose; too tight; too heavy; too light; too red; too dotty; too blue; too spotty," and so on. Her image of the old hat had become so ingrained in her self-image that she could not see herself any differently. Ms. Berenstain Bear left the store the same way she entered, wearing the same old hat.

Thus, this work receives its title, *Old Church, New Church*. Facing a grand opportunity for church transformation, it is my hope that the church doesn't do what Ms. Berenstain Bear did—become so attached to the old that nothing new can satisfy.

Jesus said many who are accustomed to "old wine" will say it's better than the new (see Luke 5:39). The old is better when affinities of the present more readily connect to the past than the future. We certainly should appreciate and value the past, but those emphases can also become hindrances for moving toward the future. As the church enters the "store of opportunity," she should be willing not only to look in the mirror of the past, but also get an image of her future. Unlike Ms. Berenstain Bear, my hope is that the church does not leave the store of opportunity wearing the same old hat.

Restoration of All Things

> …and that He may send Jesus Christ, who was preached to you before, Whom heaven must receive until the times of restoration of all things, which God has spoken by the mouth of all His holy prophets since the world began.
>
> —Acts 3:21

The apostle Peter proclaimed a restoration of all things in the beginning of the church. He spoke of restoration, not of the church, but of something before the church, and the birth of the church is therefore significant for the restoration of something beyond the church. The church is a vital part of this restoration.

John the Baptist preached "Prepare the way of the Lord." The disciples understood that he was like Elijah with the ministry of restoration (see Matt.17:11-13). As there had to be a restoration of things to prepare for the first coming of the Lord, so shall it be for His Second Coming. There must be a restoration of things forgotten, lost, or overlooked if the church is to prepare for the Lord. This discourse is a search for ideas and practices that may have been lost, and should thereby be restored in the church.

The focus of this study is the same as what Suzanne de Dietrich describes as the recurring motif throughout the Bible. "God's will (is) to save mankind and the world. This will has been at work since the world began, and it will continue to be operative throughout history until it has reached its final goal and God is all in all."[1]

God is the same, yesterday, today, and forever, but God moves by His Spirit in ways that are unique to times, seasons, cultures, and generations. In order to move with the workings of God, we must identify and hold fast to essential truths, but be willing to modify those truths in different ways to different generations. Therefore, how the church is changing connects to truths of God's unfolding plan, and moving toward the goal of saving humanity and the world.

The Importance of History

God speaks in history and through history. If we believe that God is with us, and working among us, then there is no time in history that He was not. Regardless of the darkness of any historic period, God has worked with His church, moving His church toward its intended purpose.

What God is doing in the world today connects to what He did yesterday. If we are to better understand this unfolding plan and purpose, we must observe trends and patterns that have unfolded throughout history. Glimpses of church history help us grasp the larger picture and therefore should help the church become decisive in not repeating the mistakes of yesterday, but learn from them and move forward.

The Bible, also a collection of historical writings, speaks of this ever-present working God. Therefore, beyond the compilation of the NT writings, God still works in and throughout history. There is nothing new under the sun, but what seems new was merely hidden in that which has already been. Therefore, what is happening to the church today, in the strictest sense, is not new, but is an unfolding of something that has already been, but only hidden.

There is a progressive revealing of God's plan in the pages of history. An examination of historical events helps us better understand God's plan, and how ideas and practices of yesterday affect the church of today. Therefore, it is also the task of this study to search out important truths and trends hidden in historical events.

The Center of History

...on this rock I will build My church, and the gates of Hades shall not prevail against it.

—Matt. 16:18

At the center of history ("His Story") is the cross. All things, past, present, and future, point to the event in history where Christ died on the cross. This event is pivotal for seeking to know God's unfolding plan for His church. Upon this solid rock, the revelation of Jesus Christ, who died and rose from the dead. He now lives among all who believe in Him, and works through them to fulfill God's plan for the world. Through this, God builds His church.

The church must hold firm to this very important truth for considerations of change. Through the redemptive work of Jesus' death on the cross, the church works with God for saving humanity and the world. History is an unfolding of this work.

Terms and Definitions

The Protestant Church in North America

Describing the Protestant church in North America is no small task. The most striking feature is the multiplicity of separate denominations and independent churches with doctrines and practices that vary with each one. It's not easy to diagnose the condition of anything that is so diverse.

This discourse seeks to identify important truths and trends as they relate to the church, recognizing the unique phenomenon of the Protestant church in church history. The author will therefore use a random selection of ideas and practices in the early church and note how they have affected ideas and practices of the Protestant church, particularly in North America.

Church

The word *church* (*ekklesia*) literally means "the called out ones." It is the body of Christ. It also means "an assembly." In its basic meaning, the term connotes the idea that something greater is present in the midst of unified believers than the sum of separated individuals not unified.

An important challenge throughout Christendom is identifying what constitutes the true church. The author does not presume that everyone who believes must agree with any other in all aspects the Christian faith, but there is a mysterious bond of all believers that sets them apart as God's people, God's church.

Throughout Christendom, tensions existed between the organized, institutional, established church with that of the hidden church. Throughout history, many professing Christians chose not to connect to any organized institutional church, but practiced their faith in ways separate from it. These make up the hidden church. Like those who fled to monasteries in the historic church, many Christians today also shun the "worldly" ways of the organized established church.

Church leaders, scholars, and believers will gain a clearer picture of the church as they notice important trends in both, the established and the hidden church. In the hope of presenting a clearer picture of the glorious church, this project wrestles with ideas for bringing both together. Each chapter describes these conditions and trends with the following sub-headings.

Old Church

Old church refers to the "old hat" condition of the present church, particularly in North American Protestant churches. The section "Old Church" seeks to identify ideas, beliefs, and practices that need reexamination. It does not necessarily mean that the things identified are wrong, but it does suggest our need to examine them to see if they hinder the church from moving forward.

Early Church

Early church seeks to identify important concepts prevalent in the church's beginnings. In "Early Church," we refer primarily to the New Testament for identifying the church's ideas and practices. It's difficult to conclude from Scripture a precise picture of how the church was in its beginnings. Letters written to individuals and local church settings addressed their unique and specific challenges. Therefore it would be presumptuous to apply biblical text in church practices today without considering the contexts they practiced them in the early church.

In addition to these challenges, it is also difficult to relate every aspect of early church life with practices in the church today. The church today practices many things that may or may not have any direct link to the Scriptures.

Historic Church

Historic church discussions are not an attempt to present a broad view of history, but instead to identify how certain ideas, beliefs, and practices in history have impacted the church today.

Until the Reformation, the established church mainly included the Roman Catholic and the Eastern Orthodox Church. However, during this period, there was also a hidden church, where believers chose not to be associated with either of these. Ideas and desires of the hidden church were seedbeds for the Reformation and later the Protestant movement. From examining trends of the historic church, the church of today should gain ideas for moving forward.

New Church

New church discussions include revisiting and examining important concepts that may have been lost in history, but reconsidered for moving the church forward. Important biblical concepts have been lost in historical trends, and movements toward restoration are yet unfinished. We shall observe how the Reformation of the sixteenth century is an unfinished work, and how the church in North American Protestantism faces an opportunity to continue what the Reformers began but did not finish.

Male Pronoun Usage

Throughout this discourse the author uses the male pronoun to refer to all persons. This does not suggest that females have not been instrumental in church development and are not essential for moving the church forward. The opposite is the case. Females have been essential and not adequately recognized throughout church history, and are very essential for moving the church forward.

Neither does the author use the male pronoun in reference to God to dismiss aspects of the feminine aspect of a nurturing and gentle God. The author simply uses the male pronoun for easier flow. Hopefully all who read this text will not miss important concepts the author seeks to address by focusing too much on male pronoun usage.

The Framework of This Discussion

We will identify selected topics from a passage that provides a glimpse of early church practices. These are not the only topics worth discussing, but they provide a working framework to proceed.

> ... "Be saved from this perverse generation." Then those who gladly received his word were baptized; and that day about three thousand souls were added to them. And they continued steadfastly in the apostles' doctrine and fellowship, in the breaking of bread, and in prayers. Then fear came upon every soul, and many wonders and signs were done through the apostles. Now all who believed were together, and had all things in common, and sold their possessions and goods, and divided them among all, as anyone had need. So continuing daily with one accord in the temple, and breaking bread from house to house, they ate their food with gladness and simplicity of heart, praising God and having favor with all the people. And the Lord added to the church daily those who were being saved.
>
> —Acts 2:40-47

In the following chart, the topics of the chapters relate to the passage above:

Passage	Topic for Discussion
gladly received his word and were baptized	Message and Mission
continued steadfastly in the apostles' doctrine	Church Authority and Leadership
ate their food with gladness, praising God and having favor with all people	Worship and Grace
fear came upon every soul, many wonders and signs	Preeminence of the Holy Spirit
continued in fellowship, in the breaking of bread, and in prayers	Church Unity
save yourself from this perverse generation	Judging the True and the False
breaking bread from house to house	Discipleship and Body Ministry
The Lord added to the church daily	Revival or Revolution

Each chapter may stand alone, and is substantive enough to provoke further discussion and research. Those in ministry leadership, those preparing for ministry in academic settings, and those who desire a better understanding of the condition of the church, will find this project informative and challenging. While some may find sections uncomfortable, others will find them refreshing. Opportunities for change include both discomfort and freshness.

I hope this discourse helps the church rise above the clouds of darkness hovering over it. Therefore, as the pilot announces to the passengers in times of flight turbulence; "Please be seated and fasten your seatbelts. We will rise above the storm and should experience a smoother ride." As the church moves forward, she may experience turbulence, but as she continues to rise, sooner or later the light and glory of the Son will break through.

CHAPTER ONE

MESSAGE AND MISSION

Then those who gladly received his word were baptized.
—Acts 2:40, 41

Go therefore and make disciples of all the nations, baptizing them in the name of the Father and of the Son and of the Holy Spirit, teaching them to observe all things that I have commanded you; and lo, I am with you always, even to the end of the age. Amen.
—Matt. 28:18b-20

Old Church Message

"THE CHURCH MUST be born again, again." Anyone who has been involved in the church over the years probably witnesses some disturbing things happening in the church. Many observe the condition of the church as it is. However, it's more challenging to conclude how the church should be. The church is changing and to better conclude how the church should be, it's important to examine where the church has been.

As we consider how the church is changing, the first thing to examine is the church's message and mission. There is a subtle perversion of the gospel in the church today. It is common that many Christians remain in church for years with little or no growth. Except in times of desperation, many are not convicted of sin and see no need to seek the Lord. These realities should cause the church to reexamine its message.

1

A Feel-Good, Non-offensive Message

In some Protestant churches in America, many are guilty of preaching "non-offensive," "feel-good messages." Preachers who are too afraid of offending others will not preach certain aspects of the gospel message. They will not use the word *sin* because it is too "offensive." Instead, more appropriate is a statement such as "We have issues." Neither do some mention the Holy Spirit. Again, this also, they consider "offensive," and exclude from their sermons. Even the mention of the cross and hell are omitted. Most disturbing is the fact that even the name of Jesus is offensive and not mentioned in many church pulpits. All of these, considered too offensive, some preachers rarely use in feel-good, non-offensive messages.

The feel-good message implicitly communicates that the gospel message should not be offensive if the church is to grow. Any church desires growth, but we must continue to ask ourselves:

- Where is the message of the cross?
- Whatever happened to sin?
- Why is the Holy Spirit treated like some unwanted stepchild?
- Are not accountability, loyalty, commitment, submission, and sacrifice also important aspects of the gospel message?

Should not the church include these even if it means some may leave the church? The message of God's kingdom is a message of grace that pricks the hearts of men and woman to "repent, and believe the gospel" (Mark 1:15).

A Religious Message

A "religious message" takes the opposite extreme of the feel-good, non-offensive message. A religious message places overemphasis on sin without applying the work of grace. The religious message may sound like the gospel message, but it's not. It emphasizes outward performance rather than addressing the condition of the heart.

With a religious message, people never feel they measure up, and therefore must work harder and harder to warrant God's grace. A religious message emphasizes performance and frustrates a believer's ability to enjoy the blessings and benefits of what God has already provided through the work of Jesus Christ.

The scribes and Pharisees promoted a religious system that hindered people from finding joy and freedom in serving God. Jesus expressed great anger in the temple when confronting this religious system (see Jn. 2:13-16).

The church must again cleanse itself from a religious system based on outward performance and omitting the weightier matters that deal with the heart. Confronting the religious message will free believers to know the righteousness, peace, and joy of receiving God's grace.

The Self-Help Message

The "self-help message" focuses on helping people with their problems. Anyone in ministry should desire to help others and therefore will preach messages intended to help them. Self-help messages focus on using biblical principles to bring change in a person's life. These self-help messages often appeal to ideas for finding success and happiness through right steps and formulas.

Teaching biblical principles for helping others find solutions to their problems is commendable. However, the message of the cross and its work in the believer's life must remain central to the gospel message. As Jesus was willing to go to the cross, believers must be willing to take up the cross daily as Christ's witnesses. However, the cross, which represents suffering, sacrifice, and death, does not find its place in our images of success and happiness.

Therefore, instead of focusing on a self-help message, our messages should focus on finding satisfaction in doing the will of the Lord. Teaching biblical principles and adopting them into our lives are important. However, these principles must point toward the will of the Lord, which also entails cost, suffering, and sacrifice. Happiness and success are mere by-products of our submitting to the will of the Lord. Our submitting often leads to sacrifice and suffering. This is the work of the cross and it leads to true happiness, fulfillment, and success.

The Faith Message

What many call "the faith message" has left an indelible imprint upon the church of today. The faith message has taught believers the importance of confessing God's Word for activating God's promises. These messages have emphasized using the Scriptures in areas of healing, prosperity, success, and power. The church today has benefited greatly from the faith message, but revisiting it is also important for moving forward.

One important truth not heard enough in the faith message is that faith also involves a process. This faith process may include having to endure great suffering, sacrifice, and hardships. It is common to hear of the goodness of God in reports of healing or receiving a blessing. These testimonies are good and should continue. However, in addition to these, faith also involves believing God in the midst of trials and hardships. The church does not include enough of these into its messages.

Many struggle with faith when facing difficult times, and their relationship with God suffers because of it. Often some believers dismiss others who experience these difficulties as having "little faith" or "no faith." Some are reluctant to share their struggles of faith because they don't understand how their struggles connect with their faith.

A quote cited by Justo Gonzales describes the attitude of salvation many have today. He writes; "Now everybody hopes to be saved by a superficial faith, without the fruits of faith, without the baptism of trial and tribulation, without love or hope, and with truly Christian practice."[2]

A look at Hebrews chapter eleven, the "Faith Chapter," describes witnesses of the faith as having endured great hardships. In some cases, these believers never received the full manifestation of those promises.

> These all died in faith, not having received the promises, but having seen them afar off were assured of them, embraced them and confessed that they were strangers and pilgrims on the earth.
>
> —Heb. 11:13

God honored their faith because they continued to believe in the midst of great oppositions. Therefore, the faith message should provide more insight into how one's faith overcomes the hard places of the Christian journey.

It is therefore important to include in the faith message the *process of faith*, evident in the time period between seedtime and harvest. The period of time from planting a seed until the time of manifestation is a process that requires great faith.

If we speak of God's blessings being manifested in health, wealth, and power, we should also proclaim that there is a death and sacrifice in planting a seed and steadfastness during the process of time. Therefore, in the process of faith believers prepare for oppositions to endure and overcome. This is their testimony of faith and should be included in faith messages.

The Gospel Message

This gospel often preached in American churches is that Jesus is Savior. As important as this is, it is secondary to a higher purpose. Jesus Christ is also King and all of creation becomes subject to His government in the kingdom of God.

Many know Jesus as Savior, but do not acknowledge Jesus as Lord of their lives. Jesus as Savior keeps believers from the penalty due them because of sin. However, Jesus as Lord demands submission to Him. Receiving Christ at salvation or new birth is the beginning of learning to live under God's government where Christ is King.

Marc Lawson describes how the message of salvation has taken priority over the message of the kingdom and how the idea of local church membership has taken precedence over kingdom citizenship. He writes, "While America has heard the truth that 'Jesus saves,' not all Americans have yet heard that 'Jesus reigns!'" [3] Lawson continues;

> The gospel is not only an invitation, but also a declaration of a Kingdom that is here today, not coming some day or "in the sweet bye and bye." Most American preaching and teaching focuses on the church rather than the Kingdom....While the local church and ministries can be built, the Kingdom cannot. It can only be recognized, unlocked, and acknowledged. Jesus is Lord whether anyone acknowledges it or not.[4]

A Message that Creates a Passive People

Many believe preaching the gospel is something only preachers should do. The gospel must not only be proclaimed from the pulpit, but should also involve the simplicity of heartfelt convictions of all believers speaking, testifying, persuading, exhorting, proving, convincing, and giving witness to the resurrected Lord.

The gospel of the kingdom came to set people free. It's a message that proclaims the reign of God in the believer's life. As persons surrender to Christ, they also receive a commission to give witness to the resurrected Lord. All believers who receive Christ have a mandate to share the good news by preaching the gospel. However, the message today has emphasized preaching from the pulpit and created a passive people in the pew.

As we consider the gospel message during periods of the early and historic church, an important observation is in noticing how the gospel moves individuals to commit to do God's will, and how this same commitment often brings friction in the church. The church in many ways created a religious system to restrain this freedom and to some degree these restraints continue to affect the church today. Let's examine the early and historic church to observe how the message has changed and how this change continues to affect our church messages.

Early Church Message

The work of grace through the cross is the center of the message, and how Christ the King reigns with His body, the church, is unfolding in history. Our best efforts for communicating these mysterious truths are like a baby with stammering lips, trying to express something beyond our ability to clearly communicate.

"In the beginning was the Word..." (Jn.1:1). Therefore, change begins with a word. As we address the early church's message, it previews areas the church should address. These eight areas are not conclusive, but provide a working framework. As we explore them, we shall notice how things have changed since the early church, and the church of today should adhere to certain truths for becoming the perfect bride fit for her Bridegroom.

1. The Gospel Message Is About God's Kingdom

> Now after John was put in prison, Jesus came to Galilee, preaching the gospel of the kingdom of God, and saying, "The time is fulfilled, and the kingdom of God is at hand. Repent, and believe in the gospel.
> —Mark 1:14, 15

> And Jesus went about all Galilee, teaching in their synagogues, and preaching the gospel of the kingdom.
> —Matt. 4:23

Jesus did many miracles and taught many lessons. The heart of His message was the gospel of the kingdom of God. Nowhere does Jesus define the kingdom of God, but it was the emphasis of everything He taught and did. Jews expected the Messiah to come and usher in this kingdom. Many prophets of old spoke of this coming kingdom.

> And in the days of these kings shall the God of heaven set up a kingdom, which shall never be destroyed: and the Kingdom shall not be left

to other people, but it shall break in pieces and consume all these kingdoms, and it shall stand forever.

—Dan. 2:44

Jews of that day looked for a Messiah to deliver them from the control of Rome and reestablish Israel as a ruling power as in the days of King David and King Solomon. So when Jesus preached about the kingdom of God, they looked for a natural kingdom. They didn't imagine the Messiah coming to establish a spiritual kingdom.

Today there are many opinions about how to understand the message of the kingdom. It is therefore important to lay some foundation upon which this author understands and uses the message of the kingdom in this discussion.

In her book *God's Unfolding Purpose*, Suzanne de Dietrich describes significant concepts of the kingdom that provide foundation for this discourse. She describes the kingdom this way:

> The "secret of the Kingdom" is that it must be received by faith and not by sight....The Kingdom has come because Jesus has come. The kingdoms of this world are established by their splendor. But the splendor of Jesus' Kingdom is of another sort, it is established only for those who have "eyes to see" and "ears to hear." It can be recognized by faith alone.[5]

The gospel of the kingdom is more than the message of salvation. It also involves learning to live under the authority of God's domain where Christ is King. Observing natural things and assigning them as proof of God's kingdom can be misleading, but with eyes of faith, believers recognize and submit to Christ the King.

2. The Message Establishes Authority for Doctrine and Decrees

And as they went through the cities, they delivered to them the decrees to keep, which were determined by the apostles and elders of Jerusalem.

—Acts 16:4

There was a distinction between the teachings of apostles and elders from the teachings of others. The apostles and elders set precedence for what was acceptable as doctrine. This is different from today. Teachings may come from sources with little scrutiny for credibility of Christian doctrine. With the Internet and other mediums, there is no sanction by apostles and elders to determine what should be dispersed as credible teachings of the gospel.

The authority of the church happens because of the revelation of Christ's Lordship over the church. The task of the church is to proclaim His Lordship until He comes (see 1 Cor. 11:26). The mandate for church authority is to prepare the church for this return.

3. The Message Provokes Worship and the Fear of the Lord

> So great fear came upon all the church and upon all who heard these things.
>
> —Acts 5:11

Even though the definition of worship is not in Scripture, the evidence of worship is throughout Scripture. Singing is an important aspect of worship, but worship is not confined to singing. Instead, worship is an attitude of the heart that honors God's nature, attributes, ways, and claims, whether by the outgoing of the heart in praise and thanksgiving or by deeds done in such acknowledgment. To do service is also worship.

Worship comes out of an awareness and celebration of God's goodness. Giving definition to God's grace is inadequate for describing the magnitude of the mysterious workings of the Spirit in the life of the believer. *Grace* is better experienced than explained. However, in seeking to communicate God's goodness, grace was the best word the apostle Paul could find.

The original meaning of the Greek word for grace is "ultimate beauty." The Greeks enjoyed the appreciation of beauty through philosophy, sports, poetry, drama, art, and architecture, as well as the natural beauty of mountains, streams, and coastlines. When the beauty of a thing gave joy and tranquility to the recipient, it was graceful.

Paul the apostle seized upon this idea of grace and used it to express the very heart of the gospel. He used it to describe God's action as His gift of salvation through Jesus Christ to all who believed. This grace is utter generosity of God's goodness, which acts wholly out of loving concern for the human need.[6]

Among other definitions, according to *Vine's Expository Dictionary*, grace (*charis*) has connotations as "a favor done without expectation of return; loving-kindness; unearned favor or reward; a blessing or gratuity; good will and kindness to another." Grace is the free unmerited favor and enabling power of God upon humanity. All of God's goodness is according to His grace.[7]

As a celebration of grace, the attitude and expression of worship comes out of embracing a loving devotion to please the Lord and a deep respect for His righteous judgments. When these are present in the church, worship happens, and persons become increasingly aware of God's goodness being present among them. Mysterious and wonderful workings of grace then happen among them.

4. The Message Acknowledges the Holy Spirit for Revealing the Lord

> And with great power the apostles gave witness to the resurrection of the Lord Jesus. And great grace was upon them all.
>
> —Acts 4:33

The church lives as a witness of the reign of Christ that is not only coming, but now *is*. The church already participates in the new creation through the Holy Spirit. The body of Christ is a living organism where life and ability is through His Spirit. The church has a twofold nature. Through the Spirit, the church has God's life, but in the natural world, the church also is a gathering of sinful people. The Holy Spirit works through human weaknesses for revealing spiritual mysteries of the crucified Savior who is now Lord and King.

5. The Message Promotes Unity and Fellowship

> By this shall all men know that you are my disciples, if you have love for one another.
>
> —John 13:35

Jesus' cry for His church is that all believers be united (see John 17:20-26). He identifies this unity as the main attribute for being a witness to the world, "that the world may believe that You sent Me" (John 17:21).

This oneness is not a unified organized church. Instead, this unity becomes evident through love, humility, and commitment to please the Father by doing His will. Jesus prayed for unity among believers based on believers having committed relationship with Him and the Father, and this relationship extends to other members of the household of God.

Therefore, Christians demonstrate unity as they live in union with God and one another.

Unity is the church's witness to the world. Therefore, shouldn't the cry of Jesus also become the cry of the church—"that we be one"?

The idea of a united church is unheard in today's messages, probably because we don't know what to do with it. We shall observe historical trends of how this idea of unity needs further development in the church.

6.   The Message Distinguishes the True and False

And with many other words he testified and exhorted them, saying, "Be saved from this perverse generation."

—Acts 2:40

"Not everyone who says to Me, 'Lord, Lord,' shall enter the kingdom of heaven, but he who does the will of My Father in heaven. Many will say to Me in that day, 'Lord, Lord, have we not prophesied in Your name, cast out demons in Your name, and done many wonders in Your name?' And then I will declare to them, 'I never knew you; depart from Me, you who practice lawlessness!'"

—Matt. 7:21-23

Jesus came to shine light on the works of darkness, exposing Satan's work. One of Satan's most effective weapons is deception. It is no wonder that Jesus and the early apostles said many things to help believers distinguish the true from the false.

Since perversion is subtle, many believers fall into it unknowingly. Therefore, leaders in the early church not only preached Christ, they also warned of subtle forms of false ideas of Christ. These have a form of godliness, but no power (see 2 Tim. 3:5).

This form of godliness is as true today as it was in the early church. There is a subtle twisting of truth that is rampant in the church. It is so subtle that many may suspect something to be wrong, but can't identify it. As a subtle twisting, it uses a little truth, but mixes it with things not true. Many fall victim and go astray. Therefore, there must be a distinction made between true and false Christianity.

7.   The Message Makes Disciples for Body Ministry

And when they had preached the gospel to that city and made many disciples, they returned to Lystra, Iconium, and Antioch, strengthening the souls of the disciples, exhorting them to continue in the faith, and saying, "We must through many tribulations enter the kingdom of God."

—Acts 14:21-23

Jesus and the early church included the cost of discipleship in the gospel message. The message of the cross was not only that Jesus died for the sins of the people, but also those who followed Him were told to count up the cost. Therefore, the idea of salvation being free is a misrepresentation of the gospel.

Anyone who follows Christ should expect to make sacrifices and suffer persecutions. First, the sacrifice of Christ on the cross paid for our salvation. Also, when persons follow Jesus, they must pay with the sacrifice of their own self-ambitions.

Following Christ also entails becoming a disciple—growing day by day, week by week, and becoming more and more like Christ. Therefore, the believer must have a resolved mind of being willing to surrender to the work of the cross, regardless of the cost. Jesus and the early apostles declared this cost in the gospel message. So should the church today.

8. The Message Provokes Revival or Revolution

And as they went through the cities, they delivered to them the decrees to keep, which were determined by the apostles and elders of Jerusalem. So the churches were strengthened in the faith, and increased in number daily.

—Acts 16:4, 5

The gospel is like a two-edged sword, speaking freedom to those in captivity but also confronting the establishments that hold people in captivity. Growth through revival did not happen in passive environments, but instead in the midst of tension, persecution, and conflict. These tensions were essential for moves of the supernatural and the "restoration of all things."

With challenges facing various generations throughout church history, some used the gospel to emphasize some tenets of the faith while minimizing or dismissing others. In doing so, the church may be overlooking important aspects of the gospel message today. Let's observe how the message and mission of the early church unfolded throughout the historic church.

Historic Church Message

In the early part of the second century, many letters circulated throughout the Christian community, and not all originated from apostolic authority. Some were questionable as to their authenticity and credibility. Therefore, efforts for communicating the Christian message focused on apologetics to confront heretical and false teachings. From this, church leaders identified and approved certain writings for circulation.

Leaders of the church sought to crystallize certain truths in order to make a distinction between right and wrong doctrine. These evolved into establishing creeds and canonizing certain approved letters into the New Testament as we have it today.

Right Belief: Creeds and Canons

The Apostles' Creed (around 150 AD)

The Apostles' Creed, put together probably in Rome and called the *symbol of the faith,* was the first major attempt to crystallize important doctrine. The Apostles' Creed was a statement of faith used in a person's preparation for water baptism. As a "symbol of faith," the Creed became a kind of confession, not intended as a complete summary of Christian doctrine, but rather as a brief statement concerning the Trinity and the work of God accomplished through Jesus Christ.

"Symbol of faith" in this context did not have the meaning it has today. Instead, it meant a "means of recognition, such as a token that a General officer would give to a messenger, so that the recipient could recognize the true messenger." [8]

It was a symbol whereby Christians could distinguish true believers from those who followed various heretical teachings, particularly Gnosticism and Marcionism. Anyone who could affirm The Apostles' Creed was neither Gnostic nor Marcionite.

Prior to water baptism, the candidate affirmed a *statement of faith* with a series of three questions:

- Do you believe in God the Father almighty?
- Do you believe in Christ Jesus, the Son of God, who was born of the Holy Ghost and of Mary the virgin, who was crucified under Pontius Pilate, and died, and rose again at the third day, living

from among the dead, and ascended into heaven and sat at the right of the Father, and will come to judge the quick and the dead?

• Do you believe in the Holy Ghost, the holy Church, and the resurrection of the flesh? [9]

Since they baptized new believers "in the name of the Father, the Son, and the Holy Ghost," they also posed questions as a test of true faith in the Triune God.

Thus, the core of the Christian message in the early historic church emphasized ways for qualifying the essence of who Jesus was to the believer. This was important for distinguishing Christianity from false teachings of the time.

Doctrine and Philosophy, Clement of Alexandria (155-220 AD)

Since the early years of the second century, the surrounding cultures considered Christianity as barbaric and only for the ignorant and superstitious. In some cases, people outside the Christian faith could commit crimes against Christians and not be punished because such crimes were ignored. Thus, in the early years, Christianity struggled to become a viable religion in society.

Therefore, in addition to protecting the message from heretical teachings, seeking to prove Christianity as a credible religion was important. Clement of Alexandria is worth noting for fusing together ideas of Christian doctrine with those of philosophy. He demonstrated that well respected philosophical ideas supported Christian doctrine.

Clement was not a pastor, but rather a thinker and a searcher for truth. His main goal was not to expound the Christian message for those in quest of deeper truth, but to convince pagan intellectuals that Christianity was not the absurd superstition that some claimed it to be.

Clement was convinced that there is only one truth, and therefore any truth found in Plato is the same truth revealed in Jesus Christ and in Scripture. According to him, "philosophy has been given to the Greeks just as the Law has been given to the Jews. Both have the purpose of leading to the ultimate truth, now revealed in Christ."[10]

In seeking to present Christianity along with the great philosophers of the Greeks, Clement wrote, that the Scriptures are like allegories. Thus, the Scriptures have more than one meaning. The literal meaning ought not to be set aside, but there are more revelatory meanings hidden behind the literal and obvious. Those who are content with the obvious are like children who are content with milk. However, those who desire deeper revelation must search it out with philosophical standards.

Clement's accomplishments do not lie in the manner in which he understands one doctrine or philosophy, but rather that his work is characteristic of that period. His idea for using philosophy to support Christian doctrine has greatly impacted the course of theology practiced in many seminaries today.

Council of Nicea and the New Testament Canon

Canon simply means a "measuring line, rule, sacred writings admitted to the catalog according to rule... a standard to judge by; criterion." The New Testament canon was thus a list of letters and writings officially accepted by the church as having successfully passed the criteria for legitimacy, and are inspired writings for the church.

From the time of the first apostles, many writings circulated throughout Christian communities. The Arian controversy (318 AD) was one false doctrine that provoked the church to crystallize Christian doctrine and canonize certain writings into the New Testament. Eusebius among other church leaders was significant for this endeavor.

Eusebius, a historian and a leader at the Council of Nicea (325 AD), established drafts that led to decrees for making distinctions from the heretical teachings of Arius, who denied that Jesus Christ was the eternal Son of God. By the end of the second century, core books of the New Testament were recognized. These included the Gospels, Acts, and the Pauline epistles. They agreed upon other books in the second half of the fourth century and compiled them into what we call the New Testament.[11]

St. Augustine's Ideas of Sin and Free Will

St. Augustine was another who greatly impacted the message of the church. He was born in 354 AD in North Africa. Augustine, known as the champion of free will, affirmed that God created the human will and is therefore good. However, the human will is capable of making its own decisions, and can produce evil. The origin of evil, as believed by Augustine, occurs in the bad decisions made by both humans and angels who have fallen. Augustine was therefore able to affirm both a good God who created all things and the reality of evil in the world.

Augustine also described the will as powerless against the hold sin has on it. The will is not truly free because it is not always its own master.

The power of sin is such that it takes hold of the human will, and as long as we are under its sway we are in bondage and cannot rid ourselves of it. The continuous struggle to rid oneself of sin only proves that the human will is powerless against sin.

Augustine was the last of the great leaders of the imperial church. His death was the end of an era. The New Testament Canon was in place. Important creeds were established. Essentials for Christian practices were in place. Augustine's writings became the most influential and most quoted of the Roman Catholic Church and later the Protestant churches of the sixteenth century. Even to this day, Augustine's theology touches the church in many ways.

The message of the next period in church history had little or no respect for freedom of the will. Instead, loyalty to the established church became paramount, and lack of respect for freedom of the human will and individual convictions later became a point of contention for the Reformers.

What Happened to Repentance? The Dark Ages (400-1400)

Even though letters and writings had been accepted and compiled in the New Testament, translation of the Bible into the language of many believers had not taken place. Most depended upon the priest to read and explain it. The church interpreted and explained the Scriptures in a way that lessened the importance of free will while amplifying the importance of church loyalty and participating in sacraments. Many who resisted this whole liturgical religious system and the doctrine of sacramental penance sought refuge in monasteries to practice personal devotions of pious living.

Essential practices of the early church were lost during this period. A system of religious control subdued all expressions that opposed teachings and practices of the established church. A heretic was not only a false teacher, but also anyone who opposed the church.

In 410 AD, the Goths sacked Rome, and the Roman Empire came to an end. However, the Roman Catholic Church functioned in the west, while the Imperial Church, established by Constantine, continued in the east. For about one thousand years these two institutions dominated ideas and practices of the Christian church. Church historians call this period *The Dark Ages.*

During this period, the doctrine of repentance changed into the teachings of *penance.* While repentance has the idea of changing of mind, will, and behavior; penance allows one to have regret and sorrow, but does not require change. Instead, penance required the giving of gifts to the church, doing good works, and afflicting punishment upon oneself for one's wrongs.[12]

In his book *The Unfinished Reformation,* notice how Charles Morrison describes the incredible power of religious control exerted through the church during this period.

> The essence of the Catholic penitential system—confessional, penance and indulgences.... The priest is divinely endowed with the power to forgive sins, to absolve the penitent, and to impose penalties. He stands in the place of Christ who, it is claimed, has committed this power and authority to him....The priest speaks with an ultimate authority which lifts the responsibility from the conscience of the penitent and takes into his own hands the right to dispose of the sin. He disposes of it by declaring absolution—"I absolve thee"—and by imposing penance. The penalty is graded according to the priest's judgment of the seriousness of the sin....[13]

Suffice it to say at this point, that the message of "repent and believe the gospel" (Mark1:15) as a means for receiving grace was lost during the Dark Ages. Persons believed that by submitting to the rituals and sacraments of the church, they received salvation. The Reformers challenged this idea of salvation in later years.

The Reformation Message

A resurgence of freedom of the will began in the Renaissance period of the thirteenth and fourteenth centuries. Like rebellious teenagers, many sought to find their identity by ridding themselves from their controlling parent, the Roman church. These expressions appeared in many literary works that denounced Roman church practices, and these "teenagers" sought other ways to find peace, fulfillment, and salvation. During the Reformation, Martin Luther expanded on this idea of freedom, but unlike the Renaissance rebellious teenagers, Luther sought to remain connected to the church.

The actual beginning of the Protestant Reformation in 1517 in Germany was a confluence of events with Luther's dynamic personality, considerable talent, and deep religious convictions. His personal conviction of grace by faith generated tension against the church's sacramental practices.

In a desperate search for personal peace with God, Martin Luther had found it, not in the sacraments or works of merit prescribed by the church but in Jesus Christ. He desired to reform the church with the conviction that the church had departed from its apostolic foundation.

The Reformers sought to restore two key aspects of the message that had been lost. They were "The just shall live by faith" and the "priesthood of believers." However, instead of reforming the Roman Catholic Church, they separated from it, and the Protestant movement began.

The term *Protestant* evolved to mean "One of the party who adhered to Luther at the reformation in 1529, and protested, or made a solemn declaration of dissent from a decree of the emperor Charles V....This name was afterwards extended to the followers of Calvin, and *Protestants* is the denomination now given to all who belong to the reformed churches."[14]

Key aspects of the message upon which the Reformers protested against the Roman Catholic Church are as follows.[15]

Scripture and Tradition

The single source of revelation from which the Christian church draws its teaching is the Holy Scriptures. Protestants did not reject church tradition, but highly respected tradition as an aid for the understanding of the Scriptures. The Protestant Christian seeks to understand Scripture with the assistance of all those who have labored before him. Nevertheless, Scripture itself is the final norm of Christian doctrine.

Justification by Faith

The Roman Catholic Church teaches that when Christians die they go to purgatory. They cannot expect to enter heaven until a process of expiation of their sins is complete. Only then can they expect justification and be purged from the guilt of sin.

Protestants had a different view. Righteousness is not something a person possesses, but instead God declares one to be righteous because of faith in Christ. When one believes the good news of God's love in the death, burial, and resurrection of Christ, the believer becomes righteous. Justification by faith is faith in the death, burial, and resurrection of Jesus Christ.

Certitude of Salvation

While Roman Catholic believers are confident that the sacraments are reliable to confer this grace, Protestant Christians seek certitude of salvation based on faith in Jesus Christ through the Word of God. Through faith in this work, Protestants believe this is sufficient to receive grace for salvation.

Church Sacraments

Sacrament comes from a Latin word meaning "a secret" or "a mystery." Ways and uses of sacrament differ in Roman Catholic and Protestant tradition. Roman Catholics celebrate seven sacraments, while the Protestant church recognizes two of them, communion and baptism, and more often uses the term *ordinances*.

There is for the Protestant only one means of grace: faith in the Word. But this takes many forms: obedience to the Scriptures, proclaiming the gospel, humble obedience, love for others, and others. The Reformers rejected penance as a means for receiving grace.

Priesthood of Believers

The Protestant idea of the priesthood of believers refers principally to the common right of all Christians to hear the confession of sin of one another. All Christians may be hearers to each other of God's Word of judgment and grace.

Since every Christian is a priest, there is no spiritual difference between pastor and people, but only a difference of function in the body of Christ.

"Priesthood" also speaks to the community of believers respecting each believer's authority to share in the community. A priest is not a priest to himself or herself as promoted during the Renaissance, but demonstrates priestly functions in relations to other believers.

While the message of Protestantism is not limited to the theological convictions of the early Reformers, however, these theological motifs have nevertheless remained in Protestantism. Communicating these throughout history has been to a greater or lesser degree the message of Protestantism.

Ideas freely expressed since the Reformation have greatly influenced the church's message and mission of today. One such teaching worth noting since the Reformation is that of Dispensationalism.

Dispensationalism's Influence on the Message

The viewpoint of Dispensationalism has greatly influenced the message of the church of today. These teachings emerged during the Evangelical movement.

J.N. Darby (1800-1882) is credited as the founder of Dispensationalism, although some of its ideas are from Augustine. Variety exists among Dispensationalists, but Scofield's scheme of seven dispensations is widely accepted.

Several factors of the dispensationalist influences are worth noting. First, it believes that apostles and prophets and gifts of the Holy Spirit have ceased with the forming of the New Testament.[16]

Secondly, it believes that the ministry and message of the church is namely that of sharing the message of salvation so persons will go to heaven when the Lord returns. Their view of the end-time church is the lukewarm church of Laodicea (Rev. 3). They believe there will be a remnant holding fast to the faith and Jesus will return to rescue them from total annihilation. The *Rapture* will thus rescue the church from the Antichrist and the Great Tribulation period.

Those who hold these views desire to be a part of the remnant, and therefore refrain themselves as much as possible from this "corrupt world" so as to be ready for the Rapture. Therefore, the church's role is to win as many converts as possible and save them from the world that's going down like a sinking ship.

Dispensationalist theology focuses on church quantity and not quality. Their idea of the end-time church is a weak and crippled church and that the Lord returns and raptures them before great tribulation. Persecutions and tribulations are sure to come, but dispensationalists' theology undermines the image of the church as a mature bride prepared for her bridegroom.

Dispensationalists may have difficulty with the concept of God demonstrating the power of the Spirit with signs, wonders, and miracles in the church today. Dispensationalists may also have difficulty with the ambiguities of God's progressive revelation of His purpose throughout history, since their time-line charts of the "end times" are so precise and clear. Therefore, it's important to consider how Dispensationalism has affected the church's message and mission.

New Church Message

Progressive Unfolding Revelation

Over 25 million copies of Tim Lahaye's *Left Behind* series have sold in bookstores, both Christian and secular. These are fictional stories that tell about the end times when the Rapture takes place. An important concept believed among many Christians is that the church will be snatched away one day. Yes, but before this happens the church must grow up.

God's will to save humanity and the world has been at work since the world began, and it will continue throughout history until it has reached its final goal. A challenge for understanding God's unfolding plan with His church is the fact that the Scriptures are a work of both human and divine—the Word of God and the words of men.

Men throughout biblical history encountered certain historical circumstances and wrote about those circumstances as encounters with the divine. Revelatory truths express how the divine works with human challenges for bringing salvation to humanity and to the world.

Just as God chose the humble image of the manger to reveal His Son, God continues to use the frailty of human words to reveal Himself. The center of this revelation and human history points to the cross, on Calvary, where Jesus died. Suzanne de Dietrich explains this point:

> The cross is the place where the battle between God and man reaches its climax. It is the place where God's all-powerful love wins the decisive victory over evil and death, the place where God is willing, apparently, to lose the contest in order that he may truly win it...the mystery of the cross is the focal point of all mystery that we find throughout the Bible (and throughout history), for God is nowhere more visible and nowhere more hidden than he is at Golgotha. [17]

When the apostles received Christ's command to wait for the baptism of the Holy Spirit, they did not fully understand Jesus' purpose for His church. They asked if it was time to restore the kingdom to Israel.

Ever since the Resurrection and Pentecost, the church has been in the period described as "the last days"—the time of the church. The first-century church believed in the return of Christ during their lifetime. They were diligent and preached the gospel throughout the earth (see Col.1:6).

Therefore, God's plan for the church is unfolding throughout history. The essentials of the message should remain the same, but there is a progressive movement of God's revelatory truths hidden in His purpose that each generation must seek to express.

Grace to Grow Up, Not Go Up

The early first-century church is the church's birth with all the essential elements for the church to grow and mature. God is progressively revealing Himself throughout history, including the past, present, and future. Therefore, the end-time church will not be the same as the early church, but will be the mature church, having all the key ingredients of purpose, passion, and power of the early church.

In the NT Scriptures, there are ten times more references to *growing up* than to *going up*. There are three Scriptures that speak to the church going up, and more than thirty concerning the saints' growing up.[18] Dispensationalism's teachings say very little concerning the church's need to grow up. Neither does it address the idea of the church taking an active part in "the restoration of all things" (see Acts 3:21). If the next great move of God is the Rapture, as some suppose, then an important aspect of the church to grow up is undermined.

Since the center of the Christian message is the cross, than the work of the cross must be included in the message of the church. This way of the cross is the way of salvation, but it's also the way for growing in grace to become all that God destines the church to be.

The spiritual transaction between God and the believer is the mysterious work of grace. This grace does not refer to the mysterious way the priests administered the sacraments in Roman church liturgy. On the other hand, the mysterious aspect of grace, according to the apostle Paul, is the Holy Spirit engaged in the believer for fulfilling God's plan and purpose (see Gal.5:16).

How to receive the grace and favor of God goes to the heart of the Christian message, and persons receive this grace by faith in Jesus Christ. Grace is not only for salvation in the new birth, but grace is the enabling power of God in the work and life of the church.

The apostle Paul describes growth in grace and coming to know Christ more intimately as his greatest ambition. In the Amplified version of the New Testament is an expanded rendering of Phil. 3:10a that helps us understand his life's mission:

...that I may know Him [that I may progressively become more deeply
and intimately acquainted with Him, perceiving and recognizing and
understanding the wonders of His person more strongly and more
clearly]...

—Phil. 3:10a AMP

This type of knowing Christ entails not only an initial basic knowing,
but also a progressively coming to know more and more. Ways of Christ
are infinite, and therefore knowing Him requires a continuous *coming to
know* Him. Therefore, it's not enough to believe that Jesus died on the
cross; the church must also believe in the work of the cross.

Persons come to know Christ in new birth at salvation, but in growth
to maturity believers grow in coming to know Christ more intimately. The
gospel message must not only boast in a person's need to know Christ,
but also boast in a continuous and progressive need to know Him. The
apostle states these aspects of coming to know Christ.

...that I many know Him and the power of His resurrection, and the
fellowship of His sufferings, being conformed to His death.

—Phil. 3:10

Power of His Resurrection

Knowing Christ in the power of His resurrection is foundational. The
apostle Paul was so moved by his relationship with Christ that Paul was
willing to give up all he owned, all he had learned, and all that was of
value to him. This love relationship so embraced him that it motivated
him to forgo all else. Surrendering to God's love became the compelling
and governing force of his life.

As persons experience God's love through the resurrected Lord, they
should allow that love to influence and change them. His love embraces
and captures them to continuously draw closer to Him. They, therefore,
become willing to go through whatever is necessary to know Christ
more and more.

Fellowship of His Sufferings

Knowing Christ through the fellowship of sufferings is another
level of growth. It is coming to know Christ in relations with others.
Fellowship of sufferings in commitment with others in the body of Christ
is significant for growth. Some who know Christ in the foundational level

fail to progressively know Him through the fellowship of His sufferings. This fellowship requires humility and submission to one another in the body.

This passage describes how sufferings lead to maturity.

> For it was fitting for Him, for whom are all things and by whom are all things, in bringing many sons to glory, to make the captain of their salvation perfect through sufferings.
>
> —Heb. 2:10

The believer who desires to know Christ more intimately will overcome sufferings associated with fellowship to become more like Christ. The body of Christ has not handled this idea of fellowship with Christ and with one another very well. Instead of enduring sufferings associated with fellowship, believers more commonly practice quiet separation from one another. If the church is to represent Christ more fully to the world, then it cannot dismiss the virtue of "the fellowship of His sufferings." This aspect of the gospel should be more readily included in our proclaiming the gospel message.

Conformed to His Death

There is yet a third level of growth. After believers have embraced the fellowship of sufferings, they develop into *being conformed to his death*. This happens by progressively yielding to Christ and to others in the body of Christ. When believers develop in this area of grace, they live a crucified life, and become engulfed with the plans, purposes, and power of God.

The apostle Paul describes his being conformed to Christ's death in this passage.

> I am crucified with Christ, nevertheless I live, yet not I but Christ lives in me, and the life which I now live in the flesh, I live by faith in the Son of God who loved me and gave Himself for me.
>
> —Gal. 2:20

Conclusion

In light of God's unfolding purpose throughout church history, an argument can be made that the Reformation represented the power of

His resurrection—important aspects of the church that have died were being resurrected. The next move and one the Reformers did not finish is fellowship of His sufferings. The Protestant church has embraced personal relationship with Christ, but has not embraced the fellowship of sufferings revealed through other believers. This is the next area of growth for the church.

Therefore, the faith message must cling to the cross message. The religious message must cling to the grace message. The message of Christ as Savior must cling to the message of Christ as King and Lord. The message of grace for new birth must cling to the message of growth and maturity. All of these must be included in the message and mission of the church.

Who will lead the church in coming to know Christ more and more in our relations with Christ and with each member in the body of Christ? Suzanne de Dietrich speaks of proper church authority as leading the way. She says; "The apostolic letters witness to this living development of a faith that is continually enlarged and deepened until it finally includes all the fullness of Christ in his redemptive work."[19] Church authority and leadership is our next area of discussion.

Questions for Further Research and Discussion

1. How has Augustine's theology of sin and free will affected church ideas today?

2. Are there aspects of his theology that we should revisit because they may hinder the church from moving forward?

3. What is the difference between penance and repentance, and how have these ideas affected the church of today?

4. How has Dispensationalism affected the church, and what are other important ideas for viewing eschatology?

5. Historically, how has the church communicated grace? How should the church communicate this grace, not only for salvation but also for growth and maturity?

CHAPTER TWO

CHURCH AUTHORITY AND LEADERSHIP

They continued steadfastly in the apostles' doctrine.

—Acts 2:42

Old Church Authority

My people are destroyed because they don't know me, and it is all your fault, you priests, for you yourselves refuse to know me; therefore I will refuse to recognize you as my priests.

—Hos. 4:6a TLB

WHO ARE THE guardians of the message and mission? Who models the example for others to follow? It should be spiritual leadership.

The condition of the church is a reflection of church leadership. Therefore, if we are serious about transforming the church, we must look at transforming its leadership.

In Hosea, God accused the religious leaders of keeping the people from knowing Him. While they were supposed to be leaders of righteousness, they were not. The people follow this rationale, "If the priests do it, it must be OK to do." Listed below are some important areas concerning church leadership.

Political Posturing for Position and Power

A political spirit often dominates the leadership of many churches. A political spirit is more interested in obtaining positions and power for personal gain than for serving the people of God. Oftentimes the political spirit that operates in the world finds its way in many governing board meetings of the church.

Many church governing boards have this spirit lurking among them, ready to manifest at the appropriate time to gain control of position, often for self-promotion and personal interests. This political spirit seeks authority to govern, and is willing to forfeit integrity and the freedom of the people to obtain it.

The church has for too long allowed this spirit to function. It may seem unrealistic to completely remove this spirit from the church. If not, at the least it should be recognized, confronted, and restrained as much as possible from controlling the church.

Titles, Offices, and Qualifications

Titles and offices are akin to the political spirit. In the secular arena, persons use titles to describe their professional field of expertise (i.e., judge, attorney, doctor, professor, or dentist). Often associated with using such titles is an expectation of some standard of training and preparation. Therefore, one may assume that persons with titles have been proven and are qualified by some objective standard. However, church standards vary from denomination to denomination, and with some, little or no standard is required. Therefore, the use of titles can be deceptive and misleading.

Even though different denominations have their particular standards, when one is dissatisfied with being subjected with such criteria, one can simply open another church around the corner, and is given or gives himself a title: "apostle," "bishop," or "prophet."

Giving one the title of a prophet or apostle doesn't magically release those gifts in one's life. These are gifts of grace that describe divine endowments for serving. We should honor and have a healthy respect for leaders who serve, but titles used too loosely can also include individuals not yet proven.

Lawson cites "Dangers of Riding the Title Wave," an article written by John Paul Jackson. He says;

> By giving ourselves the title of "prophet" we are yearning for distinction and recognition. But we need to beware; doing so is giving in to the subtle, religiously acceptable means of calling attention to our gift. [20]

If anyone can use such titles without any objective standard, then it weakens the value of the ministry gift when persons truly operate in them. This breeds confusion to those who may not understand that titles may not necessarily correspond to integrity, maturity, gifts, and graces for ministry. There should be a way to honor those in spiritual leadership, but the church should consider other ways than using titles.

The Office of a Bishop

It may be surprising to know that the term *office* as a position for ministry was not the idea for ministry in the early church. *Office (praxis)* refers to function, doing a deed, or serving, and not a position. The office of priest *(hierateia)* refers to the custom and function of OT priestly ministry (Luke 1:9; Heb.7:5).[21]

Ecclesiastical functions for ministry as described in the NT are bishops, deacons, and elders. *Office of a deacon* is translated *diakonia*—"...the word 'office' in the phrase 'the office of a bishop' has nothing to represent it in the original..." [22] *Office of a bishop* is rightly translated *bishopric,* which in its function connotes the idea of an elder who is mature and gifted to oversee a local congregation.

The use of the term *office* as a position carrying authority within itself is not the idea of early church authority. Instead, serving as a deacon or overseer identifies the function of ministry one serves. This idea of serving is not the same as an office or position, like the office of the president with inherited power because of its government. However, Kingdom authority is different. Jesus equates greater authority to those who are willing to serve and sacrifice for the sake of others (see Matt. 23:11).

Centralized Denominational Leadership

The strength of a denomination lies in its structure of leadership from a centralized location overseeing many congregations. However, in seeking to promote unity, doctrine, and traditions from a centralized head-quarters, the concept of God's kingdom can be undermined. Goals and objectives are set to promote the denomination, and not necessarily the kingdom of God. When denominational objectives agree with Kingdom objectives, there's no problem. However, sometimes, denominational objectives do not support, and can frustrate Kingdom objectives.

While denominations have been beneficial in the past, they face challenges to change today. There is a growing trend toward less organizational emphasis and more on spiritual connection and fellowship. This trend is a shift from denominational headquarters to a different type of leadership and oversight. These leaders will be more concerned with advancing God's kingdom than any particular denomination.

Lack of Discipline and Correction in Leadership

Who corrects the bishop? There is a place for honoring leadership, but too many congregations give unflagging allegiance to leadership and do not question their authority. In many cases when there is such reverence of titles, leaders remain in an untouchable position with little or no accountability. Therefore, bringing discipline and correction to church leaders becomes problematic.

Mark Lawson states:

> The first reason the church has lost the capacity to judge itself is because there's such a profound lack of moral authority in leadership. How can we understand true righteous judgment if we don't comprehend the fact that God called the church to judge itself and keep itself pure first? [23]

In denominations where there is a central governing body over many churches, a pastor or leader lacking proper ethical behavior simply moves to another location and repeats the same destructive behavior over and over. This is even more prevalent with leaders gifted with abilities to attract crowds or raise good offerings. Compromises allow them to continue even when their morality and integrity are questionable. It's only when civil authorities and secular media expose the issue that things get addressed. The church should better address and bring discipline to its leadership.

God never intended for church leaders to function without accountability, structure, and discipline. Just as correction happens with believers, so should it be for church leaders. However, the church continues to use leaders who reject correction. Giftedness and prestige are more esteemed than integrity and character.

Christians are now just as likely to commit adultery and get divorced as non-Christians. Christians are just as likely to steal and cheat as non-Christians. All of these signs point to church leadership and how the lifestyles they model influence people more than the messages they preach.

Our list includes just a few things to show the need for addressing church leadership. Let's now look at how church authority and leadership functioned in the early church.

Early Church Authority and Leadership

Jesus' Concept of Authority and Leadership

> It was at this time that He went off to the mountain to pray, and He spent the whole night in prayer to God. And when day came, He called His disciples to Him; and chose twelve of them, whom He also named as apostles.
>
> —Luke 6:13

Jesus spent much time in prayer before choosing His disciples. He named them apostles with the intention of sending them out for proclaiming and demonstrating the gospel of the Kingdom.

Jesus later says:

> He who hears you hears Me, he who rejects you rejects Me, and he who rejects Me rejects Him who sent Me.
>
> —Luke 10:16

Jesus' disciples continued the mission and consequently his mandate and authority. During His earthly ministry, Jesus gave His disciples a limited share of His power and authority. This authority included a direct commission to form the redeemed community, teaching them to observe all things Jesus commanded (see Matt. 28:16-20).

Early Church Authority

The church of the New Testament was built solely on the "foundation of the apostles and prophets" whose cornerstone is Christ (Eph.2:20). Apostolic leadership in the early church does not give a clear and unified picture of early church government. Though the congregation was somehow involved in important decisions (Acts 15:1; 1 Cor. 5), authoritative leadership of the apostles is obvious.

In contradistinction to the Jewish hierarchy of the OT, no one has any claim to an office through birth, but all authority and qualifications come from God (see 2 Cor. 3:5f). In the early church this authority is actually produced by the Holy Spirit (*charismata*=gifts and graces) and sometimes made known by prophecy (see Acts 13:12; 1 Tim. 1:18; 4:14); but even when conferred with the laying on of hands it is always based on the Holy Spirit (see 1 Tim. 4:14; 2 Tim. 1:6).

Rudolf Schnackenburg, a prolific writer and Roman Catholic priest from West Germany, makes some interesting observations that seem peculiar, since they contrast with Roman Catholic tradition. In his book *The Church in the New Testament*, he describes early church authority as follows:

> The gradation of rank and strict assignment of places, which also applies to the other assemblies, reveals a mode of thought that is completely alien to the Christian community....Paul is concerned in 1 Corinthians 12 precisely to overcome any attributing of different values to the various charismata, and in the next chapter he praises the sublime path of love....So even in ecclesiastical discipline, which in any case seems to be restricted to exceptional instances, the law of guidance by the Holy Spirit holds good (cf. also 1 Cor. 5), and the apostles only act as God's delegates.[24]

Therefore, what is new in the Christian community is the absolute authority of Christ with power given to those He sent (see John 2:21). For this authority, there is no privilege of birth (as with the high priest), or of intellectual formation (as with the scribes), but instead mission and endowment of grace from on high are alone the requirements.

Apostolic Authority

The early church did not use the term *apostle* to describe a religious office, but instead it was a nautical military term used to describe one sent to colonize distant lands. Later, an apostle became an official ambassador, having the authority of the government he represented. This is the idea ascribed to the twelve chosen by Jesus.

The word *apostle* originated as a military term, not a spiritual one. It literally means "to send" and applied to anyone sent with authority over another region or people. In its noun form, *apostle* referred to the function of the one being sent forth.

Lawson quotes Bill Scheidler's book *Apostles*:

> The word "apostle" was originally a seafaring term that was most specifically applied to military expectations. It at times referred to a fleet of ships and the officer that commanded the fleet. As time went on, it came to be applied to a man or group of men who were sent out on an official expedition that was authorized by the government for a particular purpose. It carried with it the idea of authorization and

commissioning by the higher power to act on behalf of that power. Its meaning grew even more specific over time as the Greeks, and later the Romans, sought to spread their cultural influence into all of the regions that had been conquered by their armies. In order to bring Greek or Roman rule to alien cultures, apostles would be authorized by the state and sent on expedition with a fleet of ships filled with colonists. These colonists would then set up a model city or colony with a model culture in the newly conquered lands. These colonies became regional centers from which Greek or Roman culture could be spread to the small cities and regions round about. In this way those nations that had been conquered militarily could be conquered ideologically and culturally as well.[25]

As such, an apostle was a true representation of the sender. The one sent was to be absolutely faithful to the purposes and intentions of the sender. In the church realm, being called an apostle was a significant designation because it meant being sent to represent the Sender, and further to advance the purposes of the King and the culture of His Kingdom.

Paul's Apostolic Authority

Paul the apostle used the term *apostle* not as a title, but to describe his mission. He did not consider himself "the apostle Paul," but instead, "Paul, an apostle."

Paul was not one of the original twelve apostles, but he defended his authority as an apostle. Paul's concept of an apostle was different from that of the Jerusalem church, where apostleship was elevated. On occasion, Paul defended his apostolic authority, because his approach to authority focused on service and sacrifice, not position and power.

Paul's idea of apostolic authority presents himself as a model to be imitated. He does not simply give commands, but leads by example, and demonstrates with his lifestyle. Those following his example should experience the same freedom he has found in Christ. Thus, through this new found sense of freedom, he proves his apostolic authority as a true representative sent by Christ.

Paul did not just preach the gospel and served his churches. He was also an apostle with authority and power to govern, and when necessary, he used his apostolic authority to correct and rebuke.

Despite his absence from Corinth he judged the case of the incestuous man, though he expected the congregation to have properly judged and excommunicated him. He says to the Corinthians, "What will you? Shall I come to you with a rod, or in love and the spirit of gentleness?" (1 Cor. 4:21).

It appears that Paul did not desire giving orders, but instead preferred exhorting and appealing to the convictions of one's freedom in Christ. He preferred not to repel by strictness, but instead to win over by gentleness. His apostolic power in no way commands anyone to follow him, but he instead pleads with others to follow him as he follows Christ.

There is unquestionably some development from Paul's general epistles to his pastoral epistles in giving instructions on church ministry and leadership. He appointed and endorsed positions of church leadership and demonstrated apostolic leadership in the churches he established.

Early Church Ambiguities

It is difficult to make out an order of church practices that prevailed in early Christian communities because they varied in place and time. Early churches were small fraternities of deep faith that banded together in worship, study, fellowship, and service. There were virtually no offices that demanded special privileges. Through the eager and voluntary services rendered, it became increasingly obvious that some members had unusual gifts and were inevitably elevated to leadership. Others served in commitment with others in Christian communities.[26]

The early church did not lack order, whether as a whole or in individual communities. These communities did not recreate order each time, but order found its base on a fundamental understanding of the Christian community finding structure and freedom through apostolic leadership.[27]

Consequently, leaders of the church, beginning with the apostles, developed into some ecclesiastical form of leadership that governed the church. It seems to have drawn partly from Jewish models, such as the ancient elders of Jerusalem, and some from pagan origin, perhaps from Hellenistic models.

There was a distinction of form in church order of Jerusalem compared to those communities beyond it. In Jerusalem, we find in the Christian community a type of hierarchy. However, Paul's apostolic leadership was different. The apostles in Jerusalem demonstrated apostolic preeminence unattainable by any other. On the other hand, Paul, the apostle, distinguished leaders mainly as instruments, servants, preachers, and messengers of Christ. The independence of the community and of individual Christians giving testimony to Christ, he thinks, has greater weight.[28]

The church according to Paul is therefore not an organization constituted in some way with order of ranks and grades, but instead is a single living organism of free spiritual gifts that serve and complete one another.

The early church is evident with a type of governmental authority that exhibits apostolic leadership. However, the people of God who with new freedom by the Spirit also recognize that church leaders are humans, who are responsible to the heavenly Chief Shepherd (See 1 Pet.5:2-4). In the early church, leadership utilizes accountability and balance.

Therefore one can conclude that in light of only glimpses of church order, apparently there is room for flexibility and freedom in governing the early church. However, some form of governmental structure eventually became essential for church order, maintenance, and sustainability.

The decisive question is whether the NT church is governed by graduated hierarchical order empowered to rule, or whether the "holy people of God" as Christian communities possess authority to establish order as led by the Holy Spirit in whatever way they find appropriate.

Throughout church history, these concepts of church government have evolved into either a hierarchical model such as in Roman Catholic traditions, or a congregational model, developed in some Protestant churches. Both have strengths and weaknesses. A model utilizing the strengths of both would prove beneficial for the church today. In search of a better model, let's consider how church government developed throughout church history.

Historic Church Authority and Leadership

Apostolic Succession and the Primacy of Peter

> "And I say to you that you are Peter, and on this rock, I will build my Church, and the gates of Hades shall not prevail against it."
>
> —Matt. 16:18

When first developed late in the second century, the principle of apostolic succession was inclusive rather than exclusive. Its claim did not concern a favorite disciple of Jesus, but instead on the witness of all the apostles.

In any case, the idea of apostolic succession came about in the historic church as an attempt to distinguish true church authority from all others. Since fellowships claiming to be Christians were sprouting up with questionable and possibly heretical teachings, the idea of apostolic succession sought to validate and ordain those leaders accepted as authentic.

The significance given Peter by Jesus as *rock* did not concern him with a fundamental and enduring position for building the church. Rather Christ Himself builds His church, and the *rock* refers to the declaration Peter made—the revelatory truth that "Jesus Christ is Lord." Instead of building the church on the personality of Peter, thereby legitimizing the primacy of Peter in apostolic succession, the concern should be on the revelation of the Lordship of Jesus Christ. Upon this *Rock*, God builds His church.

Ecclesiastical Authority with Priest and Bishops

The episcopal model finds its roots in Ignatius of Antioch, born around AD 30 or 35, who became the Bishop of Antioch. He was possibly a student of John the apostle, and was significant in shaping ecclesiastical authority and structure.

Apostles did not birth the church in Antioch, but it gave rise to a new kind of leadership. Apostolic and prophetic ministries faded out. The priest who served in sacramental rituals replaced the ministry of priesthood of believers. This new form of church leadership basically reduced Christianity to liturgical ritual in place of faith. [29]

Ignatius' seven letters were important in the development of Roman Catholic theology. He is one of the earliest writers to emphasize loyalty to a single bishop to oversee a locale (or diocese). Ignatius magnified the bishop's authority to that of representing God. Ignatius believed that wherever the bishop appears, there the people of God should be, and there is the church. Whatever has the bishop's approval is pleasing to God, and therefore it is not lawful to baptize or give communion without the bishop's consent. [30]

In contrast to Ignatius, earlier writings use bishops or presbyters interchangeably, and give the impression that there was usually more than one bishop per congregation. Apostles appointed elders to supervise the work of the church. In this respect, they fulfilled the function as bishop or overseer (*episkopos*), (see Acts 20:17, 28; Titus 1:5-9; 1 Pet. 5:1-4). Gradually one elder probably assumed the position of presiding elder. By the second century, the function of the presiding elder evolved into what we consider a bishop, one having special powers of authority and privileges.

A rigid hierarchy of church leadership with the embellishment of the three offices of bishop, presbyter, and deacon, developed further during the second and third centuries. These positions in the church received power equal to and sometimes above the state. These positions of status became seedbeds for corruption during the Middle Ages.

Priest, Clergy, and Laity

The first hint of ministry of the church as a profession appears in the writings of Ignatius of Antioch (between AD 98 and 117). He claimed the original clerics (the twelve apostles) were the bishops and the deacons (their appointed assistants).

Ogden expresses the development of clergy and laity further by saying:

> The distinction between clergy and laity did not become full-blown until the fourth century, when the church adopted a secular model. In the Greco-Roman world, the Greek word *kleros* referred to municipal administrators and *laos* to those who were ruled. As the gulf between these two grew, the *kleros* in the church became associated with the sacred, the *laos* with the secular. Since the lives of the *laos* were consumed with temporal affairs, they were perceived to be on the low rung of the saintly ladder. [31]

The role of priest as used in the Roman Catholic Church did not originate from the idea of OT priesthood. However, an official in the church is *presbuteros* which relates to *episkopos*, not *hiereus*. We are all *hieris* (priests). [32]

By the twelfth century, the separation between clergy and laity evolved to the point that many considered these as two types of Christians. *Clergy* devoted themselves to the divine office of serving the church and freeing themselves from earthly things. The others who have compromised the authentic Christian life by marrying, possessing worldly goods, and yielding to human frailties were the *laity*.

This separation led to a top-down structure of leadership. Clergy identified with ordination, being set apart for professional assignment to ministry. Laity on the other hand, became synonymous with "amateur" and "unqualified."

The Roman Catholic Church saw priestly ordination as a sacrament dedicating the person ordained to a permanent commitment for service in the church. Like baptism and confirmation, a person might be ordained only once to each of the three orders: deacons, priests, or bishops.

Ogden describes a deterioration of the believer's involvement into a passive Christian faith. He says;

> This dominance over people's lives was wedded to a theology that said that Christ had delegated to the church the right to dispense grace. Those in the hierarchy of the church therefore were in the powerful position of dispensing or withholding grace...Ordination was interpreted as a kind of second baptism that lifted the clergy into a superior stage of Christian achievement. Clerical garb symbolized their elevated status.[33]

Historic Ecclesiastical Models

Episcopate Hierarchical Authority—Roman Church Model

How did the hierarchical structure of the Roman Catholic Church continue its dominance for over one thousand years if it was not the structure practiced in the early church? What was the secret of this enormous power? Others can understand that this exercise of religious power is what the church claimed and taught both rulers and people to respect. In his book *The Unfinished Reformation,* Morrison says;

> The Church had supernatural benefits to confer and supernatural penalties to impose before which the common man and the mightiest rulers stood in awe. The penalty of exclusion from the sacraments and the threat of excommunication caused men, high and low, to tremble....The unity of the church as an institution was maintained by the tremendous claims of the papacy to possess the power of eternal life and death, symbolized by the keys of the kingdom of heaven which Christ had given to Peter and his successors.[34]

Morrison also states the Roman Catholic Church taught and practiced four basic ideas that reinforced submission to its authority:

1. Authority by administration of seven sacraments, claimed to have been instituted by Christ; the priests were uniquely endowed and entrusted to control the divine presence of grace which flows

into the physical element or action of the priest who alone is able to perform this miracle. Morrison claims that the sacraments produced a depersonalization of the individual believer. [35]

2. Authority came by passive obedience of the Catholic laity. This is closely related to depersonalization of the believer. In Roman Catholicism, the church is sharply divided into two parts—the clergy and the laity, or the people. The clergy constitutes the church, and the people passively accept the religion offered by the clergy. [36]

3. Authority by conforming to uniformity. The Roman Church claims absolute uniformity in its structure, practices, beliefs, and dogmas. Not only so, the Roman Church claims that it has maintained from the time of the apostles and of Christ himself throughout the entire history of the church.[37]

4. Authority by credibility, producing saintly characters as its witness. Since Catholicism has produced its share of saintly characters, its priesthood, monks, and nuns have committed to family life, worldly affairs and devote their lives to the service of the church, and because its people in general manifest a high degree of reverence and devotion to the church and regards these as essential to their salvation—"because of these indisputable evidences of human virtue and loyalty it is easily inferred that the moral standards of Catholicism are not only above criticism but are truly Christian." [38]

By means of an elaborate system of coercive maintenance for uniformity and loyalty, a massive army of "sacred men" swore to poverty, chastity, and obedience. The church trained them from childhood to protect and promote the church and to never doubt or challenge the authority under which their vocation depended. This army of refined hierarchical order included a body of holy men who served as priests and a separate body of holy women, nuns, who also vowed to serve the church. Both served under an infallible Pope, who they believed to derive his authority vicariously from Christ Himself, and whose power flowed down through the ranks of cardinals, archbishops, and bishops to the lowliest priest. This system governed much of the world through its system of religious coercive power and authority.

Plurality of Elders Authority—Reformed and Presbyterian Churches

Although neither the Lutherans nor the Anabaptists stressed the presbytery, John Calvin and his followers did. He believed there were in the NT four orders: pastors, doctors (teachers), deacons, and presbyters (elders), the last being primarily responsible for discipline with supervision of the individual and corporate lives of the congregation. These elders were usually civil leaders in the community. The pastor was, however, a teaching elder. Presbyterian churches still hold to this model.

Even though John Calvin identified four offices of leadership, many scholars contend that there is no clear model in the NT for ecclesiastical order and leadership. Some distinguish eldership as those mature church leaders who equip the saints to do the work of the ministry.

It is difficult to determine the biblical structure for the local church. Biblical language suggests an episcopal form of government, while at the same time making allusions to a democratic congregational form. Presbyterian churches have preferred the latter throughout their history.

Independent Autonomous Authority—Congregationalists and Baptists

Baptists practice an independent autonomous form of leadership. Baptists affirm that it should be within the authority of the local church that ministry is governed and practiced (cf.1 Cor. 12 and Eph. 4). Baptist tradition promotes the idea that New Testament church government should focus on independent local churches to reach the world. The local church is also the training center where the believer becomes equipped for his specific ministry to the world.[39]

Eventually, two offices emerged out of necessity in the Baptists' tradition, the pastor and the deacon. The pastor focuses on significant aspects of ministry such as study, praying, developing closeness with God, and delivering God's messages to His people. So pastors might be free in such endeavors, deacons serve with other matters. They help with visiting the widows, orphans, the destitute, and the sick and shut-in.

Ordination of pastors gradually arose out of the need to preserve the quality of ministry. In Baptist churches, ordination by a hierarchy of church officials has never existed. Ministers are ordained and "set apart" to preach the gospel by the approval of the local congregation, with the candidate having shown evidence that he (or she) is genuinely called of God.

Pragmatic Ecclesiastical Authority—The Methodist Model

When the Methodists organized as a church, they went about the task without any allegiance to a mandate from a New Testament pattern. Instead, they focused upon the passionate faith, ecstatic ardor, and radiance of the early church community to whom the gospel came as a message of hope. Methodism was out to restore, and was careful in establishing a structure that supported it. Church polity among Methodism does not claim to be fashioned on literal New Testament lines. It was a pragmatic approach for addressing their present needs for spreading the gospel.

John Wesley's pragmatic structure developed out of a desire to present the gospel to areas where the priests of the Church of England were not available to officiate meetings. Since communion was the very heart of Christian worship, he allowed laypersons to serve communion at these meetings.

Conflicts eventually arose because the Church of England required ordination for those who administered the sacraments. Wesley, on the other hand, concluded that since a bishop was basically the same as a presbyter or elder, all ordained presbyters, including himself, had the power to ordain others.

For some years Wesley studied the New Testament in search of the polity of the early church and determined that *bishop* and *presbyter* were identical in having biblical authority for ministry, but distinguished in terms of their functions. He concluded that the bishop's function was of a superintendent over an area including numerous local churches, while the presbyter's function was limited to the local church.

Unlike most other denominations formed by schism within Protestantism, the Methodists were already a formidable body before they became a separate church. In 1784, their societies within the Church of England included a membership of 70,000, and in the American Colonies their members estimated about 20,000.[40]

Lay Leadership Authority—Disciples of Christ Model

In 1832 at Lexington, Kentucky, two men, Alexander Campbell and Barton Stone, led their respective groups into a union to form the Christian Church (Disciples of Christ). They intended to form church government to imitate as closely as possible the church life described in the book of Acts.

They followed a congregational model of church polity that they regarded as being in accordance with NT teaching. Aligning all church practice and belief with the Scriptures became a major goal of the churches of Christ. Nothing is prescribed as an article of faith or as a requirement for communion but those things expressly taught and practiced in the Word of God, which constitutes worship, discipline, and church government.[41]

Apostleship Authority—Where's the Model?

Those who take the position that the apostolic ministry did not pass away with the first apostles use the term today to describe aspects of church government that need changing. Beyond its use in the early church, usage of the term *apostle* has been minimal. More recently, however, the term *apostle* has been associated with Pentecostal, Charismatic and nondenominational church leaders.

Pentecostal leaders such as Charles Parham, William Seymour, and John G. Lake considered their ministries apostolic because they sent thousands of their followers around the world with the Pentecostal message. Since the Pentecostal movement identified with the end-time revival and the "restoration of all things" (see Acts 3:19-21), it was not a big stretch to embrace their ministries as apostolic.

Even though mainline denominational churches have sent missionaries to various locales, they have not used the term *apostolic* to describe these endeavors. However, in *The Book of Discipline of the United Methodist Church*, the Methodist church recognizes apostolic ministry. In its section on Ordination and the Apostolic Ministry it reads:

1. The whole Church receives and accepts the call of God to embody and carry forth Christ's ministry in the world....There are persons within the Church community whose gifts, evidence of God's grace, and promise of future usefulness are observable to the community, who respond to God's call and offer themselves in leadership as ordained ministers.
2. The pattern for this response to the call is provided in the development of the early Church. The apostles led in prayer and preaching, organized the Christian community to extend Christ's ministry of love and reconciliation, and provided for guardianship and transmission of the gospel, as entrusted to the early Church, to later generations. Their ministry, though distinct, was never separate from the ministry of the whole people of God.[42]

The church's frail condition is an indication that respect for apostolic and prophetic leadership is lacking. Let's explore apostolic authoritative options for the new church.

New Church Authority: In Search of an Apostolic Model

Church Leadership and Kingdom Authority

It's a mistake to think that authority in the church equates to authority in the Kingdom. Authority in the Kingdom comes from Jesus Christ, the King, and yielding to the Holy Spirit. However, authority in the church comes from ecclesiastical governments that may or may not be yielding to the leadership of the Spirit.

Our current church system has little resemblance to New Testament church leadership.

Lawson observes:

> Most of us would be shocked to know that the New Testament only mentions the gift of "pastor" one time, "teacher" three times, "evangelist" twice, but "prophet" or "prophets" (in the New Testament context) over 60 times, and "apostle" or "apostles" over 50 times.[43]

The role of a single pastor leads most churches, and many others include denominational hierarchical structures of bishops and diocese-bishops. Church will look different when governed by a plurality of elders that includes the fivefold ministry of apostles, prophets, evangelists, pastors, and teachers. How would the church have to change to recognize apostolic, prophetic, and elder leadership teams rather than pastoral or episcopal models of leadership?

Kingdom Authority in the Church

The Kingdom of God is governed with authority. Important foundations for church authority are the Scriptures, ecclesiastical leadership, and the leading of the Holy Spirit. The Reformation began, but left unfinished, a governmental model that utilized these three for acknowledging the value of individual freedom and church accountability and loyalty.

The Reformation and Protestantism discarded the whole system in which a "sacred" man or priest presumes to act for God with divine authority over the believer's conscience. In contrast to the elaborate

Roman Catholic sacramental system for managing the moral life of the believer, Protestantism points him directly to God, and his personal relationship with God apprehends his conscience. Through faith and sincere repentance, the way to God is always open without any priestly mediator, except Jesus Christ, the High Priest.

Protestantism makes these claims, but an authoritative church model to facilitate the balance of freedom and accountability is lacking. If there is only one Mediator, then what is the place for church leaders if every believer has free access to God through Jesus Christ?

A *theocracy*, the rule of God, as some may suppose, is not the ideal model for the church because it does not acknowledge the need for guarding against the frailties and imperfections of the human element. Any form of government involving the human element is susceptible to abuse and misuse. Therefore, church government requires balance and accountability.

The task of the church today is to further develop what the Reformers started but failed to complete—a church model that acknowledges the importance of both freedom and structure. The Roman church emphasized structure, and the Reformers emphasized freedom. The recognition and bridging of these two important streams is the task for the church today. This is a part of what Morrison calls the "unfinished reformation" in his book of the same title.

Structure represented by the "law" nails down good foundational truths while life through the Spirit lifts up those truths. Structure without freedom is bondage, while freedom without structure is chaos. Both have great value in the church with Kingdom authority. A model for this concept has its base in OT tradition.

OT Models of Authority

In the Old Testament, no single entity had all authority, but there was an intertwining of three levels of authority that facilitated stability in civil and religious communities. Guardians of the message and mission were twofold: the Law and the Prophets. A third, the king, promoted civil order and provided protection.

The Law, established through Moses passed to the Leviticus priesthood. Prophets were individuals who may not have been a part of the priesthood but were called for specific times to speak on God's behalf to specific persons and groups of people. Judges and later kings primarily functioned for protection from foreign nations. All three forms of authority were essential, and this balance of power has great validity for church authority and leadership.

On the Mount of Transfiguration, Moses and Elijah appeared with Jesus, representing the law and prophets as guardians of the mysteries of the Kingdom. The church must have structure, representative of the law, and also allow freedom, representative of the prophetic. Both, the Law and the Prophets work together, pointing to Jesus Christ, the King. This model represents an intertwining structure that maintains accountability and balance.

The United States formed a government with this threefold balance of power, with the executive, judicial, and legislative branches. Even though it has minimized the possibility of dictatorship, it has also weakened concepts that reflect Kingdom authority. However, in the church, true apostles and prophets will promote Kingdom authority.

The New Testament describes the foundation of church authority in this way:

> ...having been built on the foundation of the apostles and prophets, Jesus Christ Himself being the chief cornerstone.
>
> —Eph. 2:20

Apostles and prophets continue to be essential for building the church with Jesus Christ being the chief Cornerstone. In a physical building, the cornerstone can be the main stones that provide support. The term cornerstone also has the idea of an angular stone, a tip of a pyramid. This stone is cut at the beginning, before the foundation is made, but laid last at the top when the building is complete.[44]

In the case of a cornerstone being the tip or head of a pyramid, it is like a blueprint that demands constant attention so proper alignments are made throughout the building process to ensure the tip will fit perfectly at the top. As the church is properly built, then Christ will be seen as Head of the church (see Eph. 2:20-22). Therefore, the task of apostles and prophets calls attention to the fact that all activity of the church should point toward Christ as Head and King of God's kingdom.

Individual and Corporate Authority

Church authority is based on the revelation that Jesus Christ is Lord. Therefore, every believer has a measure of authority in the kingdom of God. This authority, however, becomes evident in submitting to others in the body of Christ. This demonstrates another level of authority that extends beyond the individual to that of corporate authority.

Authority of the individual through Christ is not separate from the individual's relationship with the body of Christ. Proper spiritual authority happens within the context of Christian community. All who have a personal relationship with Jesus Christ should also seek relationship with the body of Christ, in Christian community.

It is in the fellowship of the Christian community that every believer should be fashioned to the will of God. It is within the community of the faithful that the Spirit bears witness with our spirit that we are the children of God. As the family of God, believers bond together in this fellowship.

The grace of God is directly available to every believer. However, believers do not operate in individualistic isolation because fellowship in Christian community is the mysterious medium where the grace of God flows. The living presence of Christ is among them.

Challenges for Moving Forward: Seminary Trained Leaders

As we search for an effective model for church authority, another area the church should address has to do with our seminaries and places of ministry training. In the second century, Clement of Alexandria successfully defended the Christian message by integrating concepts of Christianity with philosophy, thereby making it more acceptable in society. Through this, he also influenced methods for ministry training, integrating faith and reason into theological fields of study. This model continues to affect the church today. This approach, beneficial for the second century, needs balance for ministry training today.

Our seminaries seek to balance faith and reason. Studies in theology place greater emphasis on reason and philosophy than on the mysterious aspects of faith. Reason and philosophical arguments have their place, but not at the expense of negating the mysterious aspects where the power of the gospel is demonstrated. There are mysterious aspects of the gospel not easily explained, and therefore expressions of Christianity aren't confined to theological discourses that favor communicating truths only within acceptable philosophical constructs.

Many have difficulty communicating the mysterious aspects of the Christian faith, but demonstrate the power of the gospel with the simplicity of faith. However, many of our seminaries and places of ministry training do not offer much credibility to these.

In addition to this, philosophy alongside the introduction of critical redaction in the study of biblical text also continues to promote a divide between clergy and laity. Those who favor such study presuppose that unless one is trained in redaction criticisms, one is ill equipped to handle the biblical text. The complex procedures for explaining Scripture, they presume should be up to the "professional" minister, trained to handle such difficulties. Seminaries should therefore seek ways to include in ministry preparation not only the mental exercise of philosophy, but also the spiritual exercise of demonstration of power with the simplicity of the gospel.

Invisible Church Government, A Spiritual Approach

Proper church leadership and governmental authority will always be essential in the church. However, one does not have to look very far to recognize that church authority and leadership should change as it faces church transformation.

No human system can take the place of the Holy Spirit. No earthly denominational headquarters can replace the authority of the Spirit. The Holy Spirit as Governor has great implications as to how the church should function, and this approach requires a different type of leader.

Spiritual leaders should demonstrate authority in several ways. They experience a calling for ministry leadership, and are equipped with grace, ability, and humility recognized by others. These spiritual attributes should identify those individuals as potential leaders of the church.

One who does well within the framework of church bureaucracy may have difficulty with this leadership concept. Conversely, those who do not function well in a bureaucracy may function as great leaders within this new church concept.

The prophet Jeremiah prophesied, "And I will give you shepherds according to My heart, who will feed you with knowledge and understanding" (Jer. 3:15). Therefore, the church should recognize and appoint those leaders with a heart to please God. These leaders will guide and nurture the saints with the spirit of freedom and accountability, representing Christ with proper Kingdom authority.

In his book *Rediscovering God's Church*, Derek Prince writes of God's invisible government. He describes the structure of the church as being under the authority of the Head, Jesus Christ. Jesus is head of the church, but the Holy Spirit is Head in the church.[45]

God's invisible government, as described by Prince, is under the authority of the Holy Spirit working in and through the church, giving it the guidance and discipline needed to fulfill God's plan. Notice these passages concerning the Holy Spirit's authority in the early church:

> As they ministered to the Lord and fasted, the Holy Spirit said, "Now separate to Me Barnabas and Saul for the work to which I have called them."
>
> —Acts 13:2

> Now the Lord is the Spirit, and where the Spirit of the Lord is, there is liberty.
>
> —2 Cor. 3:17

Prince goes on to suggest that the Holy Spirit as Governor gives authority to two legs whereby the body of Christ moves. One leg of authority is apostolic teams, and the other leg is presbyteries. Apostolic teams are mainly traveling ministries given authority beyond the local church. Presbyteries, on the other hand, consist of elders (not Calvin's idea with city officials), who have been proven in character and giftedness to lead the people of God. These two legs of authority lead the church not in an organizational way but in a functioning way, where growth of the body takes precedence.

Derek Prince describes the apostolic function by saying, "Apostles were often directed to specific sections of humanity, yet they never claimed authority over single Churches."

He uses an example to describe this function.

> In a historical example, just before World War I, two men, James Saltzer and William Burton, went out from England to the Belgian Congo. In the next forty years, they established more than one thousand self-governing local Churches. All the signs spoken of in the New Testament occurred in their ministry. They were apostles to the Belgian Congo. I think apostles are sent more to a section of humanity than to a geographical area, as we see in Paul's confrontation with Peter.[46]

Apostolic teams may set up elders in local churches so each local church may be self-governed. This organization must not exist as an organizational hierarchy, but instead reflects willing relationships where members are responsible to each other for promoting the Kingdom of God. Leaders shall not lord it over the people, but instead provide guidance with proper oversight for persons to be free to give witness in their peculiar everyday affairs. Persons will be equipped and go into their areas of influence with the message and mission of Jesus in mind—carrying and demonstrating the gospel of the Kingdom throughout the world.

Prince calls this concept "revolutionary" because it captures the idea of serving an invisible God who leads His people with His authority. True Kingdom authority happens through leaders who provide structure that allows the Spirit to move in and through the church community. In the manifestation of Christ in the church—the Law and the Prophets—structure and freedom are firmly held together to point to Christ, the King.

Conclusion

If the church is going to move forward in its transformation, it will require leaders who facilitate this change. The church will benefit from an ecclesiastical authoritative structure that gives freedom to body ministry. This requires leaders having a desire to see the body of Christ function beyond the local and denominational churches to that of demonstrating the Kingdom of God.

The world is taking notice of the church. If we are to build in such a way to reflect that Christ is King, we must relate to one another appropriately. Transformation of the church requires seeking to demonstrate how the NT Christian community respects all believers. This demonstrates to the world that we are the body of Christ, where Christ is the Head.

The church is being transformed with an *invisible* form of government where the Holy Spirit is Governor of church authority. This form of government equips and guides the people of God to places of freedom where accountability expresses an attitude of humble appreciation, not submissive obligation. Therefore, the church should strive for ways to celebrate the apostolic and prophetic; church structure and individual freedom; doctrinal truths and life giving messages; missionary work and pastoral discipleship; all in the governmental structure of the new church. The next chapter develops this concept further as it explores how relating to one another in worship is a mysterious conduit of grace.

Questions for Further Research and Discussion

1. Describe attitudes of church authority that we should revisit and reexamine.

2. How should individual freedom and corporate authority work together?

3. What needs to change for the idea of an invisible government to work in the church?

4. What might be the effect for incorporating the ministry of apostles and prophets in present-day ecclesiastical structures?

CHAPTER THREE

WORSHIP, A MYSTERIOUS CONDUIT OF GRACE

...they ate their food with gladness...praising God and having favor with all the people.

—Act 2:46-47

Old Church Worship

What Does God Expect?

WITHOUT SPIRITUAL CONVICTIONS concerning worship such as in the early church, Christianity today is unlikely to remain a serious contender among world religions for impacting the world.

In his book entitled *Revolution*, George Barna mentions seven passions of the early church that he asserts should be in the church today. In his chapter "What Does God Expect?" Barna raises issues that fit this discussion concerning worship. Let's observe his findings concerning the church of today as compared to early church practices. These seven passions of the early church include:

1. Intimate Worship: Every believer was expected to worship God every day...This did not require a "worship service;" it only necessitated a commitment to feel the awe of God's magnificence, to express gratitude for His love and authority.
2. Faith-Based Conversations: The evangelistic efforts of the first believers were...low-key/high-impact conversations about truth and purpose, prayer, performing miracles to foster the

opportunity to discuss the Source of their power, and the joy-filled perspective they had toward God.

3. Intentional Spiritual Growth: Believers exhibited...and acknowledged the presence of the supernatural in their everyday adventures.
4. Servanthood: The early church served others as an expression of love.
5. Resource Investment: They shared everything together.
6. Spiritual Friendships: The church was about relationships.
7. Family Faith: Christian families taught the ways of God in their homes every day. [47]

Unfortunately, today, many believers fall short of demonstrating what was evident in the early church. From this synopsis of Barna's research, notice his observations concerning the condition of the church today.

1. *Worship*

- The biweekly service is generally the only time believers worship.
- Eight out of ten do not feel they have entered the presence of God.
- Half of all believers said they have not experienced a genuine connection or presence of God within the past year.

2. *Faith-Based Conversations*

- The typical believer will die without leading a single person to a personal relationship with Jesus Christ.
- At any given time, a majority of believers do not have a specific person in mind for whom they are praying for that person's salvation.
- Most Christians believe that since they are not gifted in evangelism, outreach is not their responsibility.

3. *Intentional Spiritual Growth*

- Only nine percent of all born-again adults have a biblical worldview. Others have a patchwork theological perspective and rarely rely upon those views for daily decisions.
- The typical believer spends less time reading the Bible in a year than engaging in other leisure activities such as watching

television, listening to music, reading other books and publications, and other things.

- When asked what constitutes success, few believers define success in spiritual terms.
- When given the opportunity to express how they wish to be known by others, one out of ten used descriptions that reflect their relationship with God.

4. *Resource Investment*

- Churched Christians give an average of three percent of their income in a typical year and feel pleased with their "sacrificial" generosity.
- Fewer than one of every ten, or 10 percent, donates at least 10 percent of their income.

5. *Servanthood*

- In a typical week, one out of four will allocate some time in serving others. Little effort is invested in serving needy people beyond the congregation.
- Most Christians who admit to having seen homeless or hurting people within the last year also admit they do not interact with them.
- The typical believer would rather give money to an organization than personally assist in alleviating the needs of hurting or homeless people.

6. *Spiritual Friendships*

- Fewer than one out of every six believers has a relationship with another believer where spiritual accountability is provided.
- The most significant influences on choices of churched believers is not teachings from the pulpit, nor advice from fellow congregants, but rather messages absorbed from the media, the law, and family members.

7. *Family Faith*

- A large majority of churched believers rely on the church rather than their family, to train their children in spiritual things.

- The likelihood of married couples who are born-again churchgoers getting divorced is the same as couples who do not profess to be Christian.
- Apart from church programs, the typical Christian family spends less than three hours per month in some joint venture developing or applying their faith.
- Most Christian parents do not believe they are doing a good job facilitating spiritual development in their children. [48]

These observations Barna highlights point to the issue of worship, which should invite the grace of God into the life of individual believers and the church community. Through worship the church becomes empowered for change.

What Is Worship?

Many people think of worship as the part of Sunday morning services where people sing songs and hymns. One prevailing attitude is that worship is for those who sing to entertain the audience. The observer doesn't actively participate, and as Barna suggests, Sunday morning worship has little impact on many who do not feel some personal encounter with God.

However, worship is not limited to what happens on Sunday morning, but is a spiritual phenomenon that gives honor and recognition to God and creates conviction for affecting change in all areas of the believer's life.

From having new awareness of the Spirit, the early church was motivated with urgency, focus, and determination, to live as the people of God. In celebration and devotion to God, believers offered sacrificial service and thereby became recipients of the benefits of such celebrations.

Worship as a spiritual phenomenon is the imparting of spiritual awareness into the individual, thus making the Christian community, the temple of God, a "spiritual building" whereby spiritual sacrifices are offered and true worship takes place. The Father seeks such to worship Him (see John 4:23).

Therefore, worship is a mysterious interchange of the Holy Spirit working through expressions of devotion that invites God's favor. Worship becomes a meaningful exercise of celebration for the people of God. Thus, worship is a mysterious conduit of grace.

Evidence of Worship

Believers claim to worship the One and Only True God through whom Jesus Christ is the Way. Therefore, worship to the One True God is essential. Worship, however, takes on many forms, not only throughout church history, but through varied expressions during Sunday morning church services, and daily lifestyles that reflect a desire to please God. Regardless of style, the core of worship should acknowledge and invite the presence of God to favor His people and "move" among them.

As Barna suggests, many people do not feel they have had spiritual encounters with God in church services. This could be because there is little reverence and respect for the things of God.

This discussion on worship does not promote ideas of religion where behaviors are changed and attitudes are not. Instead, attitudes of reverential celebration have great value for attracting the presence of God, and people change from having encountered His presence. Let's observe ways of worship in the early church.

Early Church Worship

The church of the NT is a worshipping community. Believers are fellow citizens of the saints (in heaven) and members of God's household. Through the Spirit, each has access to worship the Father (see Eph.2:8f).

It's difficult to ascertain a thorough picture of ways of worship in the early church; however, some are worth noting. Early church worship found its matrix in Jewish traditions, but with new and distinct elements. At its core is the idea that Christians live in the period of eschatological fulfillment where the death, burial, and resurrection of Christ has ushered in a new era. The stamp of early church worship was the conviction that the resurrected Lord was present among them, making them distinct and unique.

Despite local differences, common themes clearly stand out: faith in Jesus the Messiah and Lord, baptism and Eucharist, apostolic preaching and instruction, high regard for brotherly love, and eschatological expectations. In the differences practiced from place to place, freedom of worship in the early church is evident.[49]

Early church worship services featured spontaneity rather than structured and orderly forms of worship. There were variations as well as common practices throughout each worshipping community. During these services there was also vivid awareness of the Spirit being manifested through His charismatic gifts (see 1 Cor.12:4ff.; 1 Cor.14: 26f., Rom. 12:6ff.).

They Celebrated Communion

> Upon meeting in Solomon's temple and from house to house, they
> broke bread and ate meals together.
>
> —Acts 2:46

Communion is the central act of early Christian worship. It appears
that believers celebrated communion regularly in private houses, possibly
every day, or on the first day of the week (see Acts 2:46, 1 Cor.11:20).
Believers considered it a "love feast," or an expression of brotherly love
and commitment for one another.

Judging from the excesses that Paul seeks to correct, this celebration
exhibited something of a festive character. Believers celebrated with an
ordinary meal where all participated. It appears that members brought
food and shared it with others, thus showing a community of love and fellowship. There was also a blessing spoken over the cup (see 1Cor.10:16).

Communion services probably included exhortations, a common
meal, and prayers. An atmosphere of gladness and expectations testified
to its eschatological awareness of already having experienced the joy of
salvation, and yet looking forward to the "restoration of all things" at
the soon return of Christ the King (see Acts 3:20f.).[50]

The celebration of communion emphasized a giving of thanks. It was
peculiar in commemoration of their Lord and in fulfillment that He was
among them. Communion intrinsically bound them together in *koinonia*—the redeemed community that celebrated having things in common.

Communion therefore affirms commitment because of the *koinonia*.
Its place in worship as a sacrament has become the focus of the Roman
Catholic Church and some Protestant churches. The Eucharist as a
sacramental mode for possessing and dispensing a means of grace is an
important thought for further development in the history of the church.

They Baptized Believers

> Then Peter said to them, "Repent and let every one of you be baptized
> in the name of Jesus Christ for the remission of sins; and you shall
> receive the gift of the Holy Spirit"…Then those who gladly received
> his word were baptized.
>
> —Acts 2:38, 41

Baptism is the Christian rite whereby new believers confess their faith
in Christ and are initiated into the body of Christ. The early church from

the beginning practiced baptism "in the name of Jesus Christ" (see Acts 2:38; 10:48; 19:5; 1 Cor. 1:13, 15). It was not a mere rite to incorporate the believer visibly and legally into the community (see Acts 2:41), but it was a type of regeneration (see Tit. 3:5), the becoming of a new person (see 1 Pet. 1:23) who is "birthed by the Spirit from above" (see John 3:3, 5).

As a sign, baptism is a break with the past and an entrance into the Christian life. The believer by faith becomes dead to his former life and raised to a new life in Christ. In the new life, the believer becomes aware of distinguishing between "mine" and "Thine," and begins seeing things from God's perspective.

Throughout church history, the rite of baptism has been interpreted both as a sacrament essential for salvation and as merely a sign of one's commitment to Christ. As a sign, new Christians identify with the death, burial, and resurrection of Jesus Christ. In the Scriptures, there is no apparent gap between the time a person confesses Christ and the time of baptism. Therefore, some practice baptizing believers as soon as possible.

On the other hand, John the Baptist ridiculed the Scribes and Pharisees who came to him during baptism. John said, "Bear fruits worthy of repentance" (Luke 3:8). Even though John the Baptist had no intention of baptizing the religious leaders, there is an indication that he insisted that some evidence of true repentance was necessary before baptism.

Another understanding of baptism consists of teaching basic Christian doctrine for becoming a disciple. In this case, prior to baptism new converts participate in some form of training.

By the beginning of the third century, it was required that all who desired baptism be prepared with three years of training. One would receive instructions on Christian doctrine and demonstrate signs of true repentance and conversion. Before baptism, believers answered a series of questions by which they affirmed their faith in Jesus Christ.[51]

Probably our earliest reference to baptism outside the NT is in the *Didache*, a set of teachings that were foundational in many Roman church practices. Here the mode is not baptism in Jesus' name, but clearly a tri-immersion in the name of the Father, Son, and Holy Spirit. Also according to the *Didache*, baptism by "a pouring on" of water was allowed if sufficient water was not available. It seems clear that up until about the end of the fifth century, adult believer's baptism was the normal practice of the church.[52]

Whether baptism is immediate or delayed, regardless of form or practice, baptism since the early church has been an important aspect of worship and a rite for initiating new converts into the Christian community.

They Proclaimed the Word

Proclaiming the good news of the resurrected Lord is another aspect of worship, being a mysterious conduit of grace. Since writings of the New Testament had not been canonized, those who proclaimed the good news used Old Testament passages to declare that Jesus, who died on the cross and was raised from the dead, was the promised Messiah Old Testament prophets foretold.

Just as Jesus proclaimed God's eschatological message of good news (see Isa. 52:7), and announced the Kingdom of God (see Mark 1:14f.), He charged His disciples to proclaim this message also (see Luke 10:9). After Resurrection Sunday, Jesus the Messiah as resurrected Lord became central to the message. Believing on Him through the preaching of this good news became essential for salvation (see Acts 3:15; 5:31). God used this message to pierce the hearts of the hearers, and many believed the gospel (see 2 Cor. 5:20). Unfortunately, we have no details about the nature of such sermons, except that of the centrality of the cross and the resurrection of Christ.

They Prayed, Praised, and Prophesied

> Whenever you come together, each of you has a psalm, has a teaching, has a tongue, has a revelation, has an interpretation. Let all things be done for edification.
>
> —1 Cor. 14:26

Spontaneous prophetic songs and sayings of thanksgiving were central components of worship services in the early church. Prophetic speech played a large part in worship celebrations. It found expression in different ways including predictions regarding the future (see 1 Cor. 14).

The apostle recommends that prophets should speak, but no more than two or three, and that in succession (see 1 Cor. 14:29ff). He that prophesies speaks to men for edification, exhortation, and comfort (see 1Cor. 14:.3). In this way the early church acknowledged that prophetic sayings came directly from the Holy Spirit, and they esteemed prophets before teachers (see 1 Cor. 12:28; 14:11).

The apostle also warns the early church that even though prophecy is important, the church must not exaggerate its importance. There is no proof that the early church recognized prophetic utterances as words of the Lord or incorporated them into the gospels. Neither is there any mention in the New Testament of prophecy becoming a basis for instruction and doctrine. However, the Christian community is built up on the foundation of the apostles and prophets—sound doctrinal teachings from the apostles and prophetic utterances edify the church (see Eph. 2:20; cf. 3:5).

They Brought Gifts and Offerings

Every man according as he purposes in his heart, so let him give, not grudgingly, or of necessity: for God loves a cheerful giver.

—2 Cor. 9:5-8

Upon the first day of the week let every one of you lay by him in store, as God hath prospered him.

—1 Cor. 16:2

Bringing gifts and offerings is also a form of worship whereby God demonstrates grace. The church distributed a part of these gifts among the poor, the needy, and widows. The body shared other parts. "They had all things in common."

They Served Faithfully

When a person committed to Christ in the early church, that person depended upon the Christian community for survival. It was common that family members from Judaism excommunicated those who became Christian. Thus, the everyday affairs of taking care of widows and addressing the welfare of all in the community were no small tasks. This work required faithful service of all believers.

Serving also included reaching out to others and engrafting them into the community. A witness of love for one another became appealing to those who were not yet included in the community. Serving in Christian community gave witness to commitment to Christ and was another form of worship.

The ways of worship listed above are some practices of the early church, but are not the exclusive means for receiving God's grace. Worship, being spiritual, has many ways of expression. These also include the exercise of faith, love, obedience, humility, holy living, sacrifice, a grateful attitude, respect for the things of God, and other Christian virtues. In mysterious ways, these invite the presence and grace of God into the life of Christian community.

Ways for receiving grace have historically become a point of discussion for the church. The Roman Catholic Church and Orthodox Church utilized *sacraments* for administering grace. In its basic meaning, "sacrament" is a mysterious ritual, ceremony, or oath that produces obligations. It came to mean an outward and visible sign of inward spiritual grace.[53] Limiting grace to these liturgical forms became common practice for some, but problematic for others. Let's observe these tensions showing how various ways of worship unfolded throughout church history.

Historic Church Worship

As we search for the historical development of the Protestant church, an understanding of sacraments in the Roman Catholic Church provides foundation for understanding this development. *Sacrament*, as used in this form, is limited to the seven essential ways of the Rome church. Receiving sacraments was the means for receiving grace. On the other hand, not receiving sacraments placed one in imminent danger and judgment.

In contrast to early church spontaneity of worship in church services, the historic church shows significant change. Signs of development in standardizing worship are evident in the *Didache*. These include changes from spontaneous ways of worship described in the earlier letters of Paul to a more ordered pattern of worship form where the sacraments play a vital role.

Sacraments and the Roman Catholic Church

Roman Catholic Church's attempt to infuse the mystery of grace into the life of the believer with the sacraments was a worthy effort, but the Reformers believed the sacraments became more of a hindrance than a help. The whole liturgical life of the Roman church revolves around the sacraments. Seven were practiced: Baptism, Confirmation or Chrismation, Eucharist, Penance, Anointing of the Sick, Holy Orders, and Matrimony.

The Roman church taught that these sacraments are "efficacious" signs of grace—that have power within them to produce the desired results. Instituted by Christ and entrusted to the church, the sacraments dispensed grace to those who receive them.

Though not every individual has to receive every sacrament, the church affirms that, as a whole, the sacraments are necessary for salvation. Through each of them, Christ bestows a particular grace, such as incorporation into Christ and the church, forgiveness of sins, or consecration for a particular service.

The church teaches that the effects of grace come *ex opere operato*, by the very fact of being received, regardless of the personal holiness of the minister administering them. However, a recipient's own lack of proper disposition to receive the grace conveyed can block the effectiveness of the sacrament in that person. The sacraments presuppose faith and the ritual element, and nourish, strengthen, and give expression to the believer's faith. Below are brief descriptions of four of the seven sacraments.

Roman Church Baptism

Baptism is the first sacrament and given for Christian initiation. In the Roman Catholic Church, baptism is usually conferred today by pouring water three times on the recipient's head while reciting the baptismal formula: "I baptize you in the name of the Father and of the Son and of the Holy Spirit" (see Matthew 28:19).

This sacrament frees the person from original sin and all personal sins, and from the punishment due to them. Baptism causes the person to share in the life of God through a "sanctifying grace." It imparts the virtues of faith, hope, and charity and the gifts of the Holy Spirit, marking the baptized person with a spiritual seal that indicates permanent belonging to Christ.

Roman Church Eucharist

St. Ignatius of Antioch, whose teachings strongly influenced the Catholic Church, stressed the value of the Eucharist, calling it a "medicine of immortality." Ignatius wrote in his letter to the Smyrnaeans:

> Take note of those who hold heterodox opinions on the grace of Jesus Christ which has come to us, and see how contrary their opinions are to the mind of God.... They abstain from the Eucharist and from prayer because they do not confess that the Eucharist is the flesh of our Savior Jesus Christ, flesh which suffered for our sins and which that Father, in his goodness, raised up again. They who deny the gift of God are perishing in their disputes.[54]

The Eucharist, the third sacrament after baptism and confirmation, completes Christian initiation, by which Roman Catholics partake of the Body and Blood of Jesus Christ and participate in His sacrifice. The Eucharist is the source and high point of God's sanctifying action on the believer. So important is it that participation in the Eucharistic celebration is obligatory on every Sunday and holy day of obligation, and receiving it is also recommended on other days.

Roman Church Penance

The Sacrament of Penance is the first of two sacraments of healing. Different names are associated with it, calling it the Sacrament of Conversion, Penance, Confession, Forgiveness, and Reconciliation. It is the sacrament for spiritual healing needed for a baptized person who has become distant from God because of sins committed. When a person sins after baptism, he is not baptized a second time but receives the Sacrament of Penance.

While it may be helpful to confess to another, only a priest has the power to administer the sacrament for absolution. Absolution takes away sin, but it does not remedy all the disorders sin has caused. The sinner must still recover his spiritual health by doing something to make amends for the sin. He must "make satisfaction for" or "expiate" his sins. This satisfaction is *penance.*

Roman Church Holy Orders

Holy Orders include the sacrament a man receives to become a bishop, a priest, or a deacon. Holy Orders are reserved for baptized men only. "Insofar as priestly and episcopal ordination are concerned, the Roman Catholic Church teaches that this requirement is a matter of divine law, and thus doctrinal and unchangeable."[55] A bishop administers the sacrament, and is given the mission to teach, sanctify, and guide in the care of churches.

In light of the sacraments, administration of a sacrament is invalid if the person acting as minister does not have the necessary power (as if a deacon were to celebrate Mass). They are also invalid if the required "form" is lacking. Obvious cases are administration of a sacrament by a priest under penalty of excommunication or suspension, or an episcopal ordination without a mandate from the Pope.

Thomas Aquinas and the Sacraments

The Theologian Thomas Aquinas solidified the importance of sacraments in his *Summary of Theology*, written 1265–1274. He wrote this as a manual for beginners and a compilation of all of the main theological teachings of the time. It contained a summary of theological support for the Doctrine of Sacraments.

The doctrine of the sacraments follows the Christology; the sacraments "have efficacy from the incarnate Word himself." They are not only signs of sanctification, but bring it about...[56]

In a single statement, Aquinas identifies the effect of the sacraments as the means for infusing grace into the recipient. The sacraments therefore become the instruments through which the operation of Christ's justifying grace passes to believers.

Growing Tensions for Change

Tensions for change have historically been in some way connected to a search for new ways of worship. This was the case leading up to the Renaissance and Reformation. Following the breakdown of monastic institutions in late medieval Europe, accentuated by the "Babylonian Captivity" of the Roman Catholic sacramental system, the fifteenth and sixteenth centuries saw the fomenting of a great cultural debate about religious reforms and fundamental religious values.

A search for new ideas favored the notion that religious doctrine and philosophical arguments laid out by Thomas Aquinas are insufficient. In Germany, new ways of devotions caught on with university students, in search of a redefinition of God. The search moved toward accepting God as a Ruler, and not a rational governing principle. Expressions of worship would become more fervent and emotional.

Thus, a revival of Augustinian theology emerged, stating that man cannot save himself by his own efforts, but only by the grace of God. This eroded the legitimacy of the church's rigid institutions and sacramental rituals.

Led by Erasmus, the humanists condemned various forms of corruption within the church. Erasmus believed that true religion was a matter of inward devotion rather than outward symbols of ceremony and ritual. He used the ancient texts, the Scriptures, for favoring moral reforms and de-emphasizing didactic rituals. While priests emphasized works of religiosity, the respectability of the church began diminishing. Erasmus laid the groundwork for Luther.

The Reformation Response, "Grace by Faith"

The noticeable beginning of Reformation came when Luther nailed his *Ninety-Five Theses* on the door of the All Saints' Church, where persons placed notices for university-related announcements. Some points of contention were the sacraments as a means of grace, celibacy as a requirement of clergy, and the authority of the Pope. The most controversial point centered on the practice of selling indulgences and the church's policy on purgatory.

While in Roman Catholicism persons achieve justification and sanctification through the sacraments, the Reformers' "grace by faith" and "the priesthood of all believers" contradicted Roman Catholic teachings.

The Reformers distinguished the true church by two qualities: (1) the word of God rightly proclaimed, and (2) the sacraments rightly administered.[57] The central concern was the means of grace and how one may receive it.

Instead of using the term *sacraments,* Protestants on some occasions prefer using the term *ordinances.* Also, instead of focusing on seven, as in the Roman Catholic Church, Protestant churches celebrate two: baptism and communion.

For Protestants, the connection between grace and faith is central for the believer. As the sinner believes in God through Christ, grace is active for forgiving sins and being reconciled to God. Through grace, the believer continues to trust in the Lord, and demonstrates this through continuous witness and celebration of God's goodness.

Protestants and Roman Catholics have used various adjectives to describe the mysterious workings of grace in the life of the believer. Listed below are some examples.

- *Actual Grace* as used by the Roman Catholics describes the supernatural help given to avoid sin and do good works.
- *Habitual or Sanctifying Grace* as used by Roman Catholics describes God's power to assist men in performing righteous acts. For Protestants, it describes the sanctifying work of the Holy Spirit in the life of the believer.
- *Irresistible Grace* as used by Calvinists describes the sovereign work of God in regeneration and conversion.
- *Prevenient Grace* as used by Roman Catholics to refer to God's work in the heart of the baptized infant. For Protestants, it describes God's secret, preparatory work in the heart of a sinner before he believes in Christ.

The Protestant movement placed less emphasis on liturgy and the sacraments and more on personal devotion and pious living. While most Protestants celebrate baptism and communion, those who focused on the spiritual element like George Fox, founder of the Quaker movement, did not even practice these. He feared that physical things such as water, bread, and wine would draw attention away from the spiritual elements of worship and grace altogether.

New Church Worship

It is not the intention of this discourse to describe how worship looks. This would suggest that grace only works in certain practices in church services. However, in seeking to accentuate the intermingling of the natural and spiritual in ways that celebrate the workings of God in human affairs, essential aspects of worship are evident.

A re-look at ideas concerning worship would address many of Barna's concerns facing the church. Even though ways of worship are different in various local settings, it is a worthwhile pursuit toward creating a greater awareness among believers for having experienced God's presence.

This list of characteristics could be endless, but instead of focusing on the Seven Sacraments of the Roman church or the two ordinances as emphasized among Protestant churches, the focus of worship is where believers respect and celebrate God's goodness and are empowered and changed by God's grace. Key concepts of worship include these listed below.

Worship Is Spiritual

Worship as sacramental realism does not admit to any magical conceptions for the believer, but instead, worship simply forms a bond with the Lord and other believers that also demands an obligation toward holy service and commitment (see 1 Cor. 10:1-13).

It is essential to note that it is in this broad area of being spiritual that the Holy Spirit manifests Himself in the life of the church. The working of the Holy Spirit has been controversial in the church. Suffice it to say at this point that the working of the Spirit is in some way involved in the mysterious workings of grace.

Dr. Cho describes how this grace works through communion and fellowship with the Holy Spirit. He says:

> The measure of our faith is in direct proportion to our communion with the Holy Spirit. Through the communion of the Holy Spirit, we receive spiritual blessings and we tell Him our earnest desires. Though the grace of Jesus Christ and the love of God may abound immeasurably in

heaven, they are useless to us if they do not reach us. Likewise, though our hearts are full of earnest desires, if the Holy Spirit does not help us commune with God through prayer, we cannot pray properly.[58]

Worship Happens in Fellowship with the Spirit

Dr. Cho goes on to describe two key words associated with communion. (This is not communion as used in the Eucharist, but instead one being in fellowship with the Spirit.) In a worshipful experience, fellowship begins with the intercourse of friendship with the Spirit. Individuals in personal devotions or corporate settings may have fellowship—an intercourse of friendship with the Holy Spirit. Dr. Cho describes it this way:

> Without fellowship with the Holy Spirit, there can be no spiritual life, no faith with power and victory. The early church was abundant with fervent prayer, overflowing passion, rich vitality and thanksgiving, gushing out like a spring as a result of their fellowship with the Holy Spirit.[59]

How do we have this intercourse of friendship with the Holy Spirit? First, we acknowledge His Presence by speaking of Him and welcoming Him to work in our lives. Secondly, we come to spend time listening to Him in private devotions and corporate settings. Thirdly, we come to depend upon Him for guidance and power to accomplish the various tasks at hand.

These aspects of worship, therefore, are not limited to prayer and devotional meditations, but it becomes increasingly apparent that the spiritual and natural are mysteriously intertwined, and work together to impart all the benefits of grace.

Worship Happens in Fellowship with the Body

Noticeably absent from the Reformers' pursuit of the true church is the lack of development concerning "the priesthood of believers." Their language did not extend to the people of God as priests who are also mysterious vessels for releasing God's grace. The Reformers affirmed this in theory but denied it in practice.

Worship also happens in fellowship with other members in the body of Christ. The church as such is God's sacramental people where grace is in the common bond of fellowship. As a body of sacramental people, the church becomes a mysterious conduit of God's grace.

"By this all will know that you are my disciples, if you have love one
for another."

—John 13:35

The church as the body of Christ points to the reality that Jesus
lives among his people, giving each member life through each member's
relationship to Him and other members of the body. Jesus dwells in each
believer and abides corporately in the midst of gathered believers. Paul
the apostle explains:

> ...and to make all see what is the fellowship of the mystery, which from
> the beginning of the ages has been hidden in God who created all things
> through Jesus Christ; to the intent that now the manifold wisdom of
> God might be made known by the church to the principalities and
> powers in the heavenly places, according to the eternal purpose which
> He accomplished in Christ Jesus our Lord.
>
> —Eph. 3:9-11

Christ is in some way incomplete without His church. Jesus is the
head, but a head needs a body. Christ by His Spirit is bringing His body
to completion. The Spirit of Christ fills the church with His life.

Worship Invites the Spirit and Empowers Believers for Witness

> Now the Lord is the Spirit; and where the Spirit of the Lord is, there
> is liberty.
>
> —2 Cor. 3:17

God's *omnipresence*—being everywhere all the time—the church readily accepts. However, God's good favors, special benefits, and blessings
of promise are not evident in everyone's life. Through worship, believers
invite God to come near and manifest His goodness to His people. A.
W. Tozer writes:

> We all should be willing to work for the Lord, but it is a matter of grace
> on God's part. I am of the opinion that we should not be concerned
> about working for God until we have learned the meaning and the
> delight of worshipping Him.[60]

> God desires to take us deeper into Himself. We will have much to learn
> in the school of the Spirit.... He wants to lead us on in our love for
> Him who first loved us. He wants to cultivate within us the adoration
> and admiration of which He is worthy. He wants to reveal to each of

us the blessed element of spiritual fascination in true worship. He
wants to teach us the wonder of being filled with moral excitement in
our worship, entranced with the knowledge of who God is. He wants
us to be astonished at the inconceivable elevation and magnitude and
splendor of Almighty God![61]

Worship empowers believers to be partners as God's witnesses. The
Holy Spirit was sent to work in partnership with believers. Effects of the
work with the Spirit intensify when He moves believers to work with
one another.

Therefore, freedom does not mean that individuals do as they
please, but instead freedom happens in committed fellowship with other
believers. Believers celebrate this freedom in corporate worship. The
church is free because of its dependence upon Christ who is its Head,
and commitment to other members who make up the body.

Worship Evokes the Fear of the Lord

The evidence of worship in the early church produces the fear of the
Lord. When there is a deep sense of awe and respect in awareness of God's
presence, it leaves an imprint with the believer beyond the experience
itself. Therefore, worship transforms believers to have a renewed sense
of conviction, purpose, and direction from having been in an atmosphere
charged with God's presence.

A sense of the presence of God, bringing with it the reverential fear
of God, is largely missing in our churches. Tozer writes: "God hates sin
because he is a holy God. He knows that sin has filled the world with
pain and sorrow, robbing us of our principal purpose and joy in life, the
joy of worshipping our God!" [62]

Tozer also writes about an experience between Benjamin Franklin
and George Whitefield that describes how people seek to live according
to their own ability and lack a fear of the Lord. Tozer writes:

They say Benjamin Franklin was such a man. He was a deist and not a
Christian. Whitefield prayed for him and told him he was praying for
him, but Franklin said, "I guess it is not doing any good because I am
not saved yet." This is what Franklin did. He kept a daily graph on a
series of little square charts which represented such virtues as honesty,
faithfulness, charity, and probably a dozen others. He worked these
into a kind of calendar and when he had violated one of the virtues he
would write it down. When he had gone for a day or a month without

having broken any of his self-imposed commandments, he considered that he was doing pretty well as a human being.

A sense of ethics? Yes.

Any sense of the divine? No.

No mystical overtone. No worship. No reverence. No fear of God before his eyes. All of this according to his own testimony. [63]

This description of Benjamin Franklin's faith (or lack thereof) is that he did not claim to be Christian. A sadder note is the prevailing attitude of many who say they are Christian. They seek to live according to their own rules without any sense of the divine, having no fear of God. Therefore, experiencing the fear of the Lord is missing and should be restored in the church.

What Does God Expect?

A. W. Tozer addresses what George Barna describes at the beginning of this chapter about worship. In light of the concern some people might have that God is giving up on us because of the depraved state in which some people live, Tozer offers this opinion:

> No. no! This is our answer to everyone in the entire human race; We have wonderful news for you! It is the good news that the God who created us did not give us up. He did not say to the angels, "Write them off and blot them from My memory."
>
> Rather, He said, "Oh I still want them! I still want them to be a mirror in which I can look and see My glory, I still want to be admired by My people. I still want My people to enjoy Me and have Me forever."
>
> When Jesus walked the earth He was the reflected glory of God. The New Testament says that He is the effulgence of God's glory and the brightness of His person. When God looked at Mary's son, He saw Himself reflected.
>
> What did Jesus mean when He told the people of His day, "When you have seen Me you have seen the Father"?
>
> He was actually saying, "When you see Me, you are seeing the Father's glory reflected. I have come to finish the work He has given Me to do."[64]

Worship is every person's reason for existence. Whether in church or out of church, in Christ or not in Christ, everyone sets his or her devotions on something. Therefore, it is imperative that the church demonstrate heartfelt devoted reverential worship to God as the One worthy of all worship.

Conclusion

Worship and grace are two words impossible to fully define and grasp, but they are probably the two most basic elements that distinguish the church. Ways of worship vary, but the sincere heart that wants to give expression begins to worship. Through worship the church celebrates the goodness of God and causes any dark clouds hovering over the church to fade.

Through the Holy Spirit, worship becomes a mysterious conduit of grace. The Holy Spirit is also impossible to fully grasp, but through mysterious ways, God makes His presence known. The topic of our next chapter addresses the mysterious and controversial workings of the Holy Spirit.

Questions for Further Research and Discussion

1. How might worship affect the challenges of the church that Barna addresses?

2. What are the advantages and disadvantages of spontaneous ways of worship as compared to more structured and organized forms of worship? Are there attributes of worship common to both styles?

3. How might worship be a catalyst for the church moving forward?

4. How might worship as the Reformers sought to describe it affect our ideas of worship today?

CHAPTER FOUR

PREEMINENCE OF THE HOLY SPIRIT

The Enabling Power of Grace

> Repent, and let every one of you be baptized in the name of Jesus Christ
> for the remission of sins; and you shall receive the gift of the Holy Spirit.
> —Acts 2:38

IN THE EARLY church, believers depended upon the Holy Spirit for guidance, help, and power. God worked through believers, empowered by the Spirit for accomplishing His will. Some works of the Spirit included strange and mysterious behaviors not easily explained; but in the early church, undeniably supernatural phenomena occurred.

The working of the Spirit is one component of church history that no person, institution, church, government, or entity has been able to completely understand. No one has a monopoly on the ways of the Spirit. Just as the preeminence of the Spirit was a vital component in the early church, the workings of the Spirit are vital for the church today. For the church to move forward, Christians must dialogue concerning attitudes and inhibitions toward the Holy Spirit.

Old Church and Holy Spirit

Spirit of Unity or Disunity

In the early church, the Spirit associated with unity; however, today movements of the Spirit often associate with conflict, fear, divisions, and separations. One reality concerning the Spirit is that persons will continue to move in mysterious ways and have subjective convictions

71

about the Holy Spirit leading them. These movements have historically caused tension with the institutional traditions of the church.

The church seems uncomfortable and ill equipped for dealing with expressions such as "freedom of the Spirit" and "being led by the Spirit." Too often negative ideas surface, namely those of "being out of control" or "being above correction and reproach." These were not the ideas of the early church.

Therefore, coming to terms with things associated with freedom of the Spirit and being accountable to the church are both necessary. This is a point for further discussion and growth needed in the church. Let's consider other ideas concerning the Holy Spirit in the church today.

Lack of Respect for the Spirit

Too often, some churches treat the Holy Spirit like some unwanted stepchild who brings shame to the family. Discussions and sermons about the Holy Spirit often provoke discomfort, confrontation, and division. Some consider sermons concerning the Holy Spirit too offensive, and therefore forbidden in some pulpits. Church leaders and seminary professors risk losing their jobs for teaching or preaching on things concerning the Spirit.

Lack of respect for the Holy Spirit is apparent when men who do not pray and worship are often the ones leading our churches. Oftentimes, women do the praying while those who make church decisions do not. Those who lead the church too often make decisions without any acknowledgment of having a relationship with the Holy Spirit.

Since recognition of the Holy Spirit was essential in the early church, the church today should be willing to explore how the Holy Spirit might be active today. Such discussions should prove beneficial in working with the Spirit and not against Him. Just as Jesus is Lord over the church, the Holy Spirit is Lord in the church.

Chaos and Confusion

The Spirit is too often associated with confusion and chaos. Some consider behavior associated with the Spirit as emotional excesses and chaotic on the one hand while on the other hand they describe churches with order and structure as being without the Spirit. Can there be a blend of order and freedom of the Spirit? Too often denominations and churches promote one at the expense of the other.

Dr. Cho quotes John A. Mackey, former dean of Princeton University's theological college and Presbyterian Alliance Theological Seminary:

> It is better to approach religion with natural feelings than to come to it with aesthetic and orderly forms without dynamic power. One of the most important problems the church of today faces is that it regards it lawful to express feelings in every field but religion. What the present church needs is to provide something which will inflame all the human passions. From the very moment the church is completely programized [sic] and depersonalized, it becomes merely a memorial of God instead of the living institution of the power of God.[65]

Dr. Cho continues:

> What is the answer to the problem he points out? Fervent fellowship with the Holy Spirit. Without it, the church naturally becomes cold; worship becomes mechanical. Faith loses the burning passion which gives a depth to our whole personality. This kind of faith is like a stove with no fire.... Knowing this, the first question the apostle Paul asked some Ephesians who appeared tired and dejected was; "have ye received the Holy Ghost since ye believed?"[66]

Speaking in Tongues

Often associated with the Holy Spirit are strange phenomena such as speaking in tongues, gifts of the Spirit, healings, miracles, signs, wonders, and the supernatural. Some say, "I can handle the Holy Spirit, but don't give me the 'tongues.'" This is probably the most controversial area.

In the early church, believers commonly practiced speaking in tongues (*glossolalia*) alongside other gifts. Today the mention of speaking in tongues creates concern because it represents chaos, confusion, and loss of control.

Even when pastors and professors believe the gifts of the Spirit are vital for the church, they do not teach them because their church's tradition or denomination has not accepted them. Exercising spiritual gifts and moving in the Spirit do not fit within their worship traditions and are therefore not welcomed.

However, many denominations that may not celebrate movements of the Spirit today do have histories associated with fervent passionate expressions of "moves of the Spirit." For reasons unclear, many of these churches and denominations have chosen to promote more organized and structured types of worshipful expressions.

Two opposing trends have developed concerning moves of the Spirit. Those who shun practices of the Spirit have labeled those who practice them as not only strange, but "the work of the devil." On the other hand, some seek strange phenomena, believing that supernatural things occur when unpredictable ecstatic moves of the Spirit are welcome.

Seeking balance of church order and ecstatic celebration has been an ongoing challenge for the church. There is great need for further discussion that begins with a premise that the church needs the Spirit to fulfill its mission. Openness in dialogue with concerns and convictions may stretch us beyond our comfort levels, but may also lead us to places where we must increasingly depend upon Him.

Much Performance, Little Passion, No Power

According to Barna's research, many who profess Christ have little or no passion for proclaiming their faith. The solution therefore is what Jesus said—effective witness happens with the power of the Spirit (see Acts 1:8). Therefore, there is a need for the church to be empowered by the Spirit. This leads to supernatural power for giving witness to the resurrected Lord.

In the early church, God confirmed His work with signs and wonders. The church must therefore acknowledge that God uses signs, wonders, miracles, and testimonies of His power for drawing attention and revealing Himself to humanity.

The Spirit of Holiness

Holiness in the church in some traditions has been associated with styles of dress and outward appearance. In addition to this, some churches have considered it "worldly" to go to the movies, play sports, watch television, drink tea or coffee, and do many other things that looked like having fun. Some of these ideas and practices have changed in the last few years, but "the Spirit of holiness" has been and will continue to be a decisive attribute of the Holy Spirit.

The progressive trend of today takes the attitude that yesterday's ideas of holiness are too legalistic because dress and outward performance receive too much emphasis. The challenge facing the church today is this: If holiness should not be associated with ideas of previous generations, then how should the church demonstrate holiness? The church must still model holiness, even though ways of previous generations may not seem relevant today.

The key word said in the presence of God is *holy*. "Holy, holy, holy... worthy is the Lamb of God to receive glory and honor!" Therefore, the word *holy* is more than an adjective. *Holiness* describes the moral purity of God. Holiness evokes an ecstatic glory that commands total attention and reverence. Therefore, holiness is not outdated, but is still required for those who desire to see God.

> Pursue peace with all people, and holiness, without which no one will see the Lord.
> —Heb. 12:14

> Therefore, having these promises, beloved, let us cleanse ourselves from all filthiness of the flesh and spirit, perfecting holiness in the fear of God.
> —2 Cor. 7:1

The glory of God's holiness is of such magnitude that we must pursue it. Glimpses of God's holiness can be overwhelming but glorious. Beyond dress and abstaining from what has been associated with "worldly" endeavors, the pursuit of holiness must again find its way in the Christian message.

Early Church and Holy Spirit

The Promise of the Spirit

Activity of the Spirit was very evident in the Old Testament as the Spirit worked through men and women to accomplish God's plan. Unlike Old Testament times of the Spirit coming upon leaders such as prophets, priest, and kings, in the new era of the church, the Holy Spirit is active in bringing transformation and power upon all who believe. After His resurrection, Jesus instructed His followers to wait in Jerusalem until the Holy Spirit comes with power (Acts 1:1-8). One hundred and twenty gathered and waited for the promise of the Spirit.

> Then Peter said to them, "Repent and let every one of you be baptized in the name of Jesus Christ for the remission of sins; and you shall receive

the gift of the Holy Spirit. For the promise is to you and to your children,
and to all who are afar off, as many as the Lord our God will call."
—Acts 2:38-39

The outpouring of the Spirit established the early church with purpose
and power. The Spirit through the church proclaims the Lord's Kingship
and hastens the day of His coming (see 2 Cor.1:22; 5:1-5.). As the gift of
God to all believers who have been baptized, the Spirit leads believers to
live holy and empowers them to fulfill their missionary tasks as witnesses
of the resurrected Lord (see Gal. 5:16-25).

In his book *The Church in the New Testament*, Rudolph Schnackenburg
writes;

> It is precisely through the Spirit which fills the whole church, that all
> its members obtain common access to the Father and become fellow
> citizens of the saints (in heaven) and members of God's household (cf.
> Eph 2:18f.). Scarcely any thought intensified the church's eschatological
> awareness and feeling of solidarity so much as this conviction of having
> received from God the gift of the Holy Spirit through the medium of
> Christ. It is the Spirit who, according to the Acts of the Apostles, guides
> the early church and its missionaries. [67]

The Spirit as the Eschatological Guarantee

> ...You were sealed with the Holy Spirit of promise, who is the guarantee
> of our inheritance until the redemption of the purchased possession,
> to the praise of His glory.
> —Eph .1:13b, 14

The outpouring of the Spirit is the evidence that the Kingdom of
God has already broken into the current age. The coming of the Spirit
is like a "down payment" or "guarantee" of greater things to come. The
eschatological outpouring is so profound that bonding with God's Spirit
is an essential feature of the church.

The Biblical NT church was distinct in being God's redeemed community because of faith in Jesus Christ. Through the death, burial, and
resurrection of Christ, God has ushered in this eschatological new age
of the Spirit. To this day the Christian confession of faith is that Jesus
Christ will not only come again as King, but the Messiah has already
come, and the coming of the Holy Spirit is proof.

In this eschatological period, since Christ's resurrection, the church is at work fulfilling God's purposes until Christ returns. The Spirit sent down is the Spirit of Jesus Christ, resurrected, exalted, and producing life, power, and strength in His church. Through the Holy Spirit, the Lord directs His earthly community, sends forth preachers, uses them to equip His church to effect its growth, gives it freedom and unity, provides strength for enduring and overcoming in the midst of persecution, and in short, leads the body of Christ in its work until the end of the age.

The workings of the Spirit, with human cooperation, guides the church in its witness to the resurrected Lord and the reality of the Kingdom of God having broken into this current age, and given a foretaste of the age to come. Believers struggle with tension and celebrate with expectation in the "already" and "not yet" of the Kingdom of God.

Authority of the Spirit

> As they ministered to the Lord and fasted, the Holy Spirit said, "Now separate to Me Barnabas and Saul for the work to which I have called them"....So, being sent out by the Holy Spirit ....
>
> —Acts 13:2,4

> For it seemed good to the Holy Spirit, and to us, to lay upon you no greater burden than these necessary things...
>
> —Acts 15:28

The authority of the Spirit governs the church to fulfill its mission. There is recognition of authority of the Spirit that causes the church to yield to His leading. Throughout the NT, happenings throughout the church community were said to be; "by the Spirit," "through the Spirit," "in the Spirit," and similar descriptions. It's as though the church did nothing without the Spirit's participation and approval.

The early church acknowledged in various ways the workings of the Holy Spirit. This didn't mean that the church waited and listened for direct instructions from the Holy Spirit without church authority and eldership. The early church practiced ministry with both freedom of the Spirit and apostolic leadership.

The particulars of how freedom of the Holy Spirit worked with apostolic authority in the early church remain nebulous and elusive. However, worth noting are two important points. First, one cannot deny that the operation of the Spirit was essential in early church development.

Secondly, the works of Holy Spirit are not easily explained, but are unquestionably evident.

Unity of the Spirit

Unity of the Spirit is probably one of the biggest challenges facing the church, but Suzanne de Dietrich provides hope in her description of how Pentecost is the witness for moving toward church unity:

> Pentecost is God's answer to the Tower of Babel. The Tower of Babel symbolizes unity created from below, on the basis of human pride that tries to lift itself up to heaven, and leads only to chaos (Gen.11). The Church's unity, by contrast, is a gift from on high; it is the work of the Holy Spirit. Men do not create this unity; all they can do is receive it, manifest it clearly, and rely upon it.
>
> The ability to speak in many languages, by means of which all races can hear the gospel, is a kind of description of what the reign of God will be like when all barriers that separate men are broken down. Pentecost marks the beginning of the vast reassembling of the scattered children of God, which the prophets had hoped (see Isa. 2:2-3; 11:10-12; 43:5-7; Jer. 31:10; Ezek. 34:11-13; cf. John 11:49-52).[68]

Suffice it to say at this point that the Holy Spirit is the Spirit of unity, not disunity, chaos, and confusion. Becoming more aware of the workings of the Spirit will enable the church to work toward this unity.

Speaking in Tongues in the Early Church

> And they were all filled with the Holy Spirit and began to speak with other tongues, as the Spirit gave them utterance.
>
> —Acts 2:4

In the early church, speaking in tongues (*glossolalia*) was a common practice. According to Paul, the apostle's teachings to the Corinthian church, not everyone spoke with tongues, but those who did thought they had received a superior gift. Paul corrected this by putting the gift of glossolalia in proper perspective.

The points of disagreement concerning tongues in the church today are at least twofold. First, some believe that it is a learned phenomenon where persons learn new languages and can articulate in different languages to persons of different regions. In this case those of foreign lands should understand the language of "tongues."

In Acts 2, persons of foreign lands heard them speak in the language of foreigners. However, this ability was not through learning the language of foreigners. Instead, this was a miraculous sign of the coming of God's Kingdom. Peter, the apostle said they were not drunk with wine, but that this strange experience was what Joel prophesied—the Spirit being poured out upon all flesh is a sign of the Kingdom (see Acts 2:14-21).

The second point of disagreement concerning speaking in tongues and other gifts is that some believe the church no longer needs them. Those with this view believe the early church needed these gifts, but since we now have the Scriptures, today's church does not need speaking in tongues and the other gifts.

On the other hand, those who believe they benefit from glossolalia ignore both of these positions. The benefits, they believe, far exceed any theological debates that seek to discredit it.

It's not the author's intention to debate glossolalia, but simply to raise it as an issue facing the church that will not quietly go away. The obvious evidence is the fact that some will speak in tongues and some will not. Speaking in tongues should not be an issue that divides the church. Paul the apostle recognized both views, and emphasized that all things should work toward edification of the body. He said:

> For he who speaks in a tongue does not speak to men but to God, for no one understands him; however, in the spirit he speaks mysteries. But he who prophesies speaks edification and exhortation and comfort to men. He who speaks in a tongue edifies himself, but he who prophesies edifies the church. I wish you all spoke with tongues, but even more that you prophesied; for he who prophesies is greater than he who speaks with tongues, unless indeed he interprets, that the church may receive edification.
>
> —1 Cor. 14:2-4

Signs and Manifestations of the Spirit

> These signs shall follow those who believe: In My name they will cast out demons; they will speak with new tongues; they will take up serpents; and if they drink anything deadly, it will by no means hurt them; they will lay hands on the sick, and they will recover... And they went out

and preached everywhere, the Lord working with them and confirming the word through the accompanying signs. Amen.

—Mark 16:17, 18, 20

But this is what was spoken by the prophet Joel: "And it shall come to pass in the last days, says God, That I will pour out My Spirit on all flesh; Your sons and your daughters shall prophesy, Your young man shall see visions, Your old men shall dream dreams. And on My menservants and on My maidservants I will pour out My Spirit in those days; and they shall prophesy."

—Acts 2:16-18

A "sign" contains part of the evidence and also points to something greater. It does not pretend to express the full reality and complete mystery of the subject to which it is pointing.

The authority of the Spirit, manifested in signs, wonders, miracles, the supernatural, glossolalia, and prophesying gives proof that the Kingdom has already come, and gives the church a foretaste of more to come. It gives witness to signs of the Kingdom that marked Jesus' ministry and also manifested in the early church.

In the book of Acts as Luke records, Peter, the apostle, did not say the prophecy of Joel is fulfilled. Instead he said, "This is what was spoken by the prophet Joel." Therefore, we can view Pentecost as a beginning of something more to come—a sign pointing to something greater.

We can make two inferences from this. First, God will not only use Jewish believers to spread His message. God will use all people. Second, God will not just speak through select leaders. God will use men and women, young and old men, from all walks of life to dream dreams, see visions, and speak prophetically concerning the Kingdom of God. There is strong evidence that suggests Pentecost was the beginning of something that will grow continually until the Lord's return.

Other Manifestations of the Spirit

The preeminence of the Spirit and the time of the church go hand in hand. In the early church, the Christian community worked collaboratively with the Holy Spirit, giving witness to the resurrected Lord.

According to Paul the apostle, other evidences include salvation, moral strength, and holy living (see Rom. 8:15, 23; 2 Cor. 1:22; 5:5). The Holy Spirit is evident in the life of each believer for bringing personal change. The Holy Spirit is the Spirit of holiness, producing holiness and morality in the life of the believer.

> For if you live according to the flesh you will die; but if by the Spirit you put to death the deeds of the body, you will live. For as many as are led by the Spirit of God, these are the sons of God.
> —Rom. 8:13, 14

The witnesses of angels and the supernatural are also manifestations of the Spirit.

> Now an angel of the Lord spoke to Philip, saying, "Arise and go toward the south along the road which goes down from Jerusalem to Gaza"....
> —Acts 8:26

Operations of the Spirit have been and will continue to be a major topic of interest. While some welcome this discussion, others hesitate. While some prefer quiet, orderly, predictable gatherings, others go to the other extreme with seemingly out-of-control behavior. The early church witnessed manifestations of the supernatural with signs and wonders. It's easy to accept the idea that God's ways are far above man's reasoning, yet we hesitate to consider how God's ways also include the mysterious ways of His Spirit.

Those uncomfortable with expressions associated with the Spirit may find acceptable ground by acknowledging the fact that the Holy Spirit is present among us and uses signs to point the church toward something greater to come. God, by His Holy Spirit, is working in and through His people to accomplish His will. We shall notice that ways of the Spirit have historically caused discomfort and tension in the church, but these tensions were essential for moving the church forward.

Historic Church and Holy Spirit

Throughout Christendom there has been ongoing stress between freedom of the Spirit and organized forms of church structures and traditions. Freedom of the Spirit emphasizes individual revelation and personal conviction, while the institutional church emphasizes structure, order, correct doctrine, and loyalty to established church authority.

Let's observe how these tensions have been apparent throughout church history. As we consider these tensions, we must recognize that the same tensions exist today, and the church will benefit by growing beyond its fears for becoming a mature church formed, led, and empowered by the Spirit.

Church History, Early Years

During the second and third centuries, bishops competed with one another for positions and power. Persecutions and ridicule of Christianity of previous years had stopped, and Christianity was finding its place in society. The rich and powerful began to enter and dominate the life of the church. It seemed that the "tares of the world" were growing so rapidly that they choked "the wheat" out of the church. This blunt reality convinced some that comfortable living was the greatest enemy of the church. A prevailing issue for those with such convictions was this: How does a true Christian be loyal to the church when the church has become so much like the world?

Prior to the third century, Christianity struggled to be an acceptable viable religion. Thus, early Christian fathers placed great emphasis on making distinctions between acceptable writings and doctrine in contrast to those deemed heretical. The struggle toward having right belief and right doctrine took precedence over individual freedoms.

From about 150 AD, the time of the Apostles' Creed, to about 400 AD, right doctrine and right belief, and receiving proper sacraments, distinguished the true from the false and validated church membership. This expression of church for the most part became the established church.

However, another segment of the church was dormant and hidden. These included believers who did not place great emphasis on right dogma but instead followed their personal convictions. They may not have used terms such as "led by the Spirit," but they moved with convictions they believed were from God. Many resisted the doctrines of the established church, and the church declared them heretical.

During this period, being a heretic did not only mean being one who followed false doctrine—it also included anyone who disagreed with established church doctrine and practice. Those who did not accept church practices were discouraged from pursuing their personal convictions. Any teachings that did not agree with the established church became grounds for punishment, excommunication, and possibly death.

Distinguishing between true and false Christianity is not the point of discussion here. Instead, the focus of this discussion is on addressing the tension between submitting to established church authority and following one's personal convictions often identified as "being led by the Spirit."

Acknowledging and respecting the tensions between the two is a challenge to this day. Combining freedom of personal convictions and loyalty to church authority is the work of the Spirit and therefore should work together. Models that accentuate both will greatly benefit the church today.

Some groups that accentuated personal convictions over form and ritual, the church considered heretical because their practices went beyond boundaries of what the church considered Christian. However, their ideas and practices are worth noting because of the thin line that sometimes existed between the true and false.

Spiritualism

The beginning of what is considered *spiritualism* is hard to trace. It emphasizes inner spiritual development. Some practices of spiritualism have gone beyond what many consider Christian, but other practices the church has accepted. Finding themselves fed up with endless debates on dogma, and worldly practices in the church, some sought refuge to develop their faith in more personal and spiritual ways.

Throughout church history, the emphasis on correct doctrine worked in favor of higher socioeconomic classes, who had greater opportunities for education. Those less educated could not discuss complicated matters of theology and were considered needing someone to protect them from doctrinal error. Thus, some showed little or no interest in doctrine and theology but instead pursued their spiritual development without these.

The spiritualist movement that began in early years and revived in the seventeenth and eighteenth centuries attracted both the educated and those with little or no formal education. They sought opportunities for personal piety and other ways of expressing their faith. This evolved into many seeking solitude as in monasteries of earlier years.[69]

Monasticism

In not being allowed to worship according to their own convictions, many fled to monasteries. These sought to keep themselves from the worldliness of the official established church. They separated themselves from the world and the church to experience a more personal and intimate dimension of spiritual life.

The Greek term for monastery (*monachos*) probably meant celibate and single, rather than alone and solitary. Monasticism was inspired by Paul's words, "that those who chose not to marry had greater freedom to serve the Lord" (see 1 Cor. 7:7, 8). Practices of monasticism originated with travelers such as the exiled Athanasius and Jerome.

Even before Constantine's time in the fourth century, some felt called to an unusual lifestyle of spiritual discipline. Origen, following Platonic ideas of seeking the "wise life," lived a life of extreme asceticism. He took literally the word of Christ by making himself a "eunuch for the Kingdom."

Although the church rejected Gnosticism, some felt its influence in the widely held notion that there was fundamental opposition between the body of the flesh and life in the spirit. Therefore, in order to live fully in the spirit, many believed, it was necessary to subdue and punish the body. Bringing discipline to the bodily passions became prominent in the monastic lifestyle.

At the core of those who sought the monastic lifestyle was a desire to experience a more spiritual life through personal devotion and piety. Their concern was that the church had become corrupt by the world, and the liturgical rituals of sacraments left many feeling depersonalized and empty. Many believed that in order to fulfill their Christian devotions, they had to isolate themselves in monastic communities, and thus separate from the world and the church that had become too much like the world.

Gonzales, a noted educator and historian, records what many did:

> Many found an answer in the monastic life: to flee from human society, to leave everything behind, to dominate the body and its passions, which give way to temptation. Thus, at the very time when churches in large cities were flooded by thousands demanding baptism, there was a veritable exodus of other thousands who sought beatitude in solitude.
>
> When the church joins the powers of the world, when luxury and ostentation take hold of Christian altars, when the whole of society is intent on turning the narrow path into a wide avenue, how is one to resist the enormous temptations of the times? How is one to witness the Crucified Lord, to the One who had nowhere to lay his head, at a time when many leaders of the church live in costly homes, and when the ultimate martyrdom is no longer possible? How to overcome Satan,

who is constantly tempting the faithful with the new honors that society offers? [70]

Another point worth noting is that those who sought the monastic life were not seeking to escape the authority of the church. In monasteries, monks had to obey their superiors. A hierarchical order clearly defined provided leadership. At the head of each housing unit was a superior, who in turn obeyed the superior of the monastery and his deputy. Therefore, those who sought the monastic lifestyle were not rejecting authority, but instead other things considered "of the world" that resided in the institutional church.

A surprising fact concerning many who desired admission in a monastery is that they were not baptized and not yet Christian. The monastery lifestyle attracted many, even pagans, to pursue the monastic spiritual lifestyle of personal piety.

Throughout church history, many pursued deeper spiritual development without looking to church leaders for inspiration and guidance. What might this say about the church's missed opportunities for reaching those who desire spiritual development, but do not look to the church?

Justification and Sanctification, Luther and Calvin

It was not Martin Luther's intention to start a movement that separated from the established Roman church, but his belief of being justified by faith moved him to stand firm on his conviction and it led to such separation. This conviction was one that dominated the Reformation Period.

Martin Luther, overwhelmed by the doctrine of justification by faith, paid little attention to sanctification. He insisted that what was important was not the manner of a life that sanctifies, but instead the grace of God that justifies.

Calvin, and the Reformed tradition, agreed with Luther on justification, but insisted that God who justifies is also the One who sanctifies. God offers to believers the power for living a holy lifestyle.

A spin-off from the Lutherans was the Moravians, who accepted Calvin's position of sanctification. The Moravians experienced tension with the Lutherans because the Moravians emphasized pietism for experiencing justification and sanctification. The Moravians were instrumental in influencing John Wesley in his belief of justification and sanctification as a two-fold work of grace in the life of the believer.

Even though the spiritualist movement (as accepted in the church) is difficult to trace, Jacob Boehme (1575-1624) is one whose experience connects with many who desire personal piety when church practices do not satisfy personal spiritual desires. His pursuit of cultivating the inner life was his reaction against the cold dogmatism of theologians, and the seemingly empty use of church sacraments.

Born of Lutheran parents, Boehme as a young boy developed a deep faith; however, long sermons, like dissertations on theological debates, caused him to lose interest. He, like many others, took responsibility for cultivating his own inner spiritual life.

Boehme emphasized moves and freedom of the Spirit over right doctrine and ceremonial practices. From these, he caused church leaders to be uncomfortable because of his visions, dreams, and other spiritual experiences. Some labeled him a heretic.

Boehme did not have many followers, but one greatly influenced by his teachings and writings was George Fox, founder of the Quaker movement.

Quaker Movement

George Fox (1624-1691), being disgusted at the worldliness of the church, concluded all the various sects in England to be wrong. In opposing the "natural reason" of the Deists, Fox believed in "the capability we all have to recognize and accept the presence of God."

On more than one occasion, Fox made the following comment:

> I was glad that I was commanded to turn people to that inward light, spirit, and grace, by which all might know their salvation, and their way to God; even that divine Spirit which would lead them into all Truth and which I infallibly knew would never deceive any. [71]

The "Quakers" were so named because those who attended their gatherings would notice enthusiastic trembling of those overwhelmed with the Spirit. When attending other gatherings, such as among the Baptists, Fox would speak out, being "so urged by the Spirit." These outbursts became more and more frequent, and church officials not only threw him out of their meetings but sometimes left him beaten and stoned.

Fox argued that ultimate truth was not in Scripture, but that ultimate truth was in the Spirit who had inspired Scripture. Fox was thus accused of blasphemy and conspiring against the government. His followers experienced persecution and were thrown in jail for blasphemy, vagrancy (wandering from place to place with no established residence), inciting riots, and refusing to pay tithes.

Notice how Gonzales describes how these freedoms clashed with established authority and the church.

> In 1664, Charles II issued an edict forbidding unlicensed religious assemblies. Many groups continued gathering in secret. But the Quakers declared that it would be a lie to do so, and therefore simply disobeyed the royal edict. Thousands were then imprisoned, and by the time religious tolerance was granted in 1689, hundreds had died in prison.... In Massachusetts, the most intolerant of the colonies, Quakers were persecuted, condemned to exile, and even mutilated and executed. [72]

William Penn, who became a follower of the Quaker movement, desired to establish a new colony in which there would be complete religious freedom. Religious tolerance, which was a part of Penn's "holy experiment," became imbedded in the Constitution of the United States.

George Fox was aware of the danger that emphasis on freedom of the Spirit would lead to excessive individualism. Other movements with a similar emphasis did not last. Fox, however, avoided this danger by also emphasizing the importance of love and community.

Boehme and Fox are just two of many historic figures who emphasized development of inner life in the Spirit, as opposed to institutional religion that focused on liturgical and ritual form, right doctrine, and theological debate. Evidences of these tensions continue to be evident in the historic church.

Pietism and Personal Responsibility

Just as spiritualists, as described above, opposed the institutional church, they also opposed each other. Movements toward individual spiritual development also espoused individualism and separatism. Since the Protestant Reformation, individual freedom with "freedom of the Spirit" and adherence to doctrine and tradition continue to display an obvious tension. Pietism sought to bridge the two together.

Pietism was a response to the dogmatism of theologians and the rationalism of philosophers, both of which seemed to contrast with the living faith that was at the heart of Christianity. Although Pietism was a German movement, it more closely associated with Calvinism than with Luther's doctrine. Philipp Jakob Spener (1635-1705) insisted that the God who justifies also sanctifies and gives believers the power for "holiness of life."

As a movement, Pietism began in the seventeenth century and emphasized good works and holy living. Gonzales comments:

> In a sense, what was at stake in the controversy over Pietism was whether the Christian faith should simply serve to sanction common morality, or should rather call believers to a different sort of life. Orthodox preaching took for granted that God requires of believers nothing more than correct doctrine and a decent life. The Pietists insisted on the contrast between what society expects of its members and what God requires of the faithful. This has always been an uncomfortable challenge for a comfortable Church. [73]

Spener's outline for the Pietist movement focused on Luther's doctrine of the priesthood of believers to suggest that the common Christian should take more responsibility for spiritual development. Therefore, every Christian should have a more intense life of devotion and study. To attain this goal, Spener suggested small groups such as his "colleges of piety."

Spener, like Luther and many who came before him, was not in opposition to the doctrines of the church, but instead insisted that preachers should set aside their polemical and academic tones that paraded the preacher's knowledge and instead, preach the gospel in such a way to call believers to obey God's Word. Spener insisted that doctrine is not to serve as a substitute for faith. What Spener proposed was another reformation of the church, or at least the completion of what had begun in the sixteenth century, but had been interrupted by doctrinal debates.

Many embraced the Pietist movement and joined the small circles or colleges of piety, even though some theologians accused the movement of being too emotional, subjective, and even heretical. Eventually in spite of such opposition, Pietism left its mark on the entire Lutheran tradition.

Historians disagree as to the nature of Pietism. Some feel it was a revival of medieval monastic and mystical piety. Others believe it represented progress in Lutheranism and looked forward to further development of the church. Whatever view one takes, without a doubt, Pietism can be credited for fostering a desire for holy living, biblical scholarship, and ministry in missions.

Methodism and John Wesley

Like Luther, Spener, and others, John Wesley (1703-1791) had no interest in founding a new denomination, but simply wanted to bring to England what Spener brought to Germany. Just as Spener clashed with the Lutherans, Wesley clashed with the Church of England. This is another example of how freedom of the Spirit clashes with beliefs and practices with the established church.

Two experiences stand out in Wesley's inner spiritual awareness. As an Anglican priest, Wesley served as a young pastor in Savannah, Georgia. On one occasion, he asked a Moravian convert for advice regarding his work as a pastor and missionary to the Indians. In his diary, he records his conversation with the Moravian convert:

> He said, "My brother, I must first ask you one of two questions. Have you the witness within yourself? Does the Spirit of God bear witness with your spirit, that you are a child of God?" I was surprised, and knew not what to answer. He observed it, and asked, "Do you know Jesus Christ?" I paused, and said, "I know he is the Savior of the world." "True," replied he; "but do you know he has saved you?" I answered, "I hope he has died to save me." He only added, "Do you know yourself?" I said, "I do." [74]

In further description of this conversation, Wesley admits that the experience left him moved, but confused. He had always thought of himself as a good Christian, having been raised in a good Christian home, and taking communion at least once a week. Back in England, he made more contact with the Moravians, and concluded that he, Wesley, lacked this saving faith. On May 24, 1738, Wesley described the experience that changed his life.

> In the evening I went very unwillingly to a society in Aldersgate Street, where one was reading Luther's preface to the Epistle of the Romans. About a quarter before nine, while he was describing the change which God works in the heart through faith in Christ, I felt my heart strangely warmed. I felt I did trust in Christ, Christ alone for salvation: And an assurance was given me, that he had taken away my sins, even mine, and saved me from the law of sin and death. [75]

Wesley, who preached for a while with George Whitefield, witnessed at their meetings people weeping and crying loudly for their sins, while others collapsed to the floor. After rising from the floor, people then expressed great joy, declaring that they felt cleansed of their sins and evil ways.

This experience was far different from what Wesley experienced through the sacraments, and moved with conviction, he felt compelled to take the gospel to unchartered westward territories of America.

Wesley, like many others, experienced the tension and conviction of following his belief while seeking to adhere to the conflicting demands of the established church. Like Luther, at the beginning of Protestantism, Methodism would succumb to separation and opposition from the Church of England. Methodism eventually emerged as a separate denomination.

Pentecostalism

While Americans were fighting the Revolutionary War and establishing independence from England, American Protestant churches were fighting for and obtaining their own independence from established denominational churches. Leading the way were the fiery Methodists. John Wesley, the founder of Methodism, many also recognize as the spiritual father of the modern holiness and Pentecostal movements.

Perhaps the most famous outbreak of enthusiastic, Pentecostal-like worship in American history occurred in the great Cane-Ridge Camp Meeting in Logan County, Kentucky in June 1800. Led by Presbyterian ministers—James McGready, William Hodges, and John Rankin, this revival continued for over a year and exhibited most of the emotional phenomena that is often characterized as Pentecostalism. This is how one described it:

> A Methodist minister, John McGee, succeeded in sparking the movement when, while preaching, he was overcome by his feelings and "shouted and exhorted with all possible energy." Soon the floor of the Red River Presbyterian Church was "covered with the slain" while "their screams for mercy pierced the heavens."
>
> Their "godly hysteria" included such phenomena as falling, jerking, barking like dogs, falling into trances, the "holy laugh" and "such wild dances as David performed before the Ark of the Lord." In some services, entire congregations would be seized by and the "holy laugh" and ecstasy which could hardly be controlled.... From 1800 until the present day such phenomena have accompanied in some degree most major revivals, regardless of denomination or doctrine. [76]

Within a decade the revival that began at Cane-Ridge in 1800 evolved with camp meetings becoming a common experience of American religious life. The man most responsible for refining the revival was Charles G. Finney. From 1843 until his death, people flocked to barns, schoolhouses, and open-air meetings to hear him preach.

Finney went further than Wesley's "second blessing of grace" to that of promoting the idea of triune salvation of spirit, soul, and body. A revival of holiness alongside baptism of the Holy Spirit became major components for the Pentecostal movement. Notice the development of emphasis of holiness and sanctification with that of baptism of the Holy Spirit:

> According to Finney, a person could achieve the coveted state of Christian perfection or sanctification by simply exercising free will and cultivating "right intentions." Sin and holiness, he explained, could not exist in the same person. [77]

Those interested in promoting the "entire work of sanctification" planned to hold another meeting in Philadelphia on June 13, 1867. Thirteen Methodist ministers from New York signed this agreement, naming themselves The National Camp Meeting Association for the Promotion of Christian Holiness. They voted to hold a camp meeting at Vineland, New Jersey, July 17 through 26, 1867. [78]

From this meeting, the modern holiness crusade began. Those who attended felt that the meeting was destined to "exert an influence over all Christendom" as well as "initiate a new era in Methodism."

Little did these men realize that this meeting would eventually result in the formation of over a hundred denominations around the world, and indirectly give birth to the Pentecostal movement. Although clearly interdenominational, the Methodists dominated the meeting.

In spite of the great popularity of the doctrine of the holiness, controversy began in the Methodist Church. There were many factors that led to controversy, but one of the most disturbing was the idea of a *come-outism movement*, which declared an anti-denominational platform.

In 1885, John P. Brooks, a loyal Methodist, left the Methodist church. He denounced the easy lifestyle of "worldly indulgences" that tolerated church parties, festivals, and dramatic presentations. During the last two decades of the nineteenth century the Methodist church faced the idea of defiant come-outism, and it forced every Methodist bishop and minister to stand with or against the holiness movement.

The tension came to its peak in 1894. The General Conference of the Methodist Episcopal Church produced a statement with the tensions of the Holiness movement in mind. It reads:

> But there has sprung up among us a part with holiness as a watchword; they have holiness associations, holiness meetings, holiness preachers, holiness evangelists, and holiness property. Religious experience is represented as if it consists of only two steps, the first step out of condemnation into peace and the next step into Christian perfection. The effect is to disparage the new birth, and all stages of spiritual growth from the blade to the full corn in the ear....We do not question the sincerity and zeal of these brethren; we desire the church to profit by their earnest preaching and godly example; but we deplore their teaching and methods in so far as they claim a monopoly of the experience, practice, and advocacy of holiness, and separate themselves from the body of ministers and disciples. [79]

Those loyal to the Methodist church now faced the agonizing decision of staying with the Methodist church or joining the come-outers in new movements. It is an interesting note that the come-outers with their emphasis on holiness did not form one large denomination, but instead they created many fragmented denominations. Between the years 1893-1899, many churches formed. The intensity of conflict within the Methodist church produced more than twenty-three separate denominations within this seven-year period.

Azusa Street Revival

A startling feature of nineteenth-century British revivals was the appearance of glossolalia, the speaking in tongues manifestations discussed earlier in this book. This phenomenon, witnessed previously at the Presbyterian Church on Regent's Square, London, in 1831, stirred more people to begin manifesting the tongues phenomenon in church services. The preacher, Edward Irving, attempted to calm the worshippers and maintain order, but his efforts failed.

America also experienced an outbreak of the tongues phenomenon during the same period as the Welsh revival. Charles Parham was the first to single out glossolalia as the only evidence of one's having received the baptism with the Holy Ghost. He taught that this phenomenon should be a part of normal Christian worship rather than a curious by-product of religious enthusiasm.

William J. Seymour, a student of Parham and leader of the Azusa Street Revival in 1907, was the first to develop a theological doctrine that glossolalia, the baptism of the Holy Ghost with evidences of speaking in tongues, was available to every believer.

Seymour believed that the holiness movement had been wrong in teaching that sanctification was also the baptism with the Holy Spirit. It was rather a "third experience" separate in time and nature from the "second blessing." Sanctification brought cleansing and purification, while baptism with the Holy Spirit brought power for service.

Seymour traveled to California. He visited holiness meetings, but when he began preaching his message on Azusa Street in an abandoned Methodist church, revival broke out. The platform of his preaching was "let the tongues come forth," and persons came from miles away to receive their own "Pentecostal experience." He proclaimed to his listeners, "Be emphatic! Ask for salvation; pursue sanctification; and seek the baptism with the Holy Ghost." These meetings were associated with seemingly uncontrolled moves of the Spirit that included miracles and divine healings.

The meetings transcended racial and cultural barriers. Whites, Blacks, Chinese, and even Jews attended and worshipped side by side to hear Seymour (a Black man) preach the gospel. What began as a local revival in a small Black church attracted people of all races from all over the nation. One exclaimed, "The color line has been washed away in the blood."

Many more radical holiness churches and missions closed their services and came to Azusa Street. Soon such physical demonstrations as "the jerks" and "treeing the devil" manifested these meetings. Before long spiritualists and mediums from numerous occult societies around Los Angeles began attending and practicing their séances and trances in the services. Disturbed by these developments, Seymour wrote Parham for advice on how to handle "the strange experiences of spirits" and begged him to come to Los Angeles and take over supervision of the revival.

The Azusa Revival continued for three years. Visitors from all parts of the nation reported their findings. Reports that an unusual outpouring of Pentecost had come to California eventually spread throughout Europe. Most of those who visited were convinced and genuinely accepted the teachings and practices they witnessed, thus experiencing their own Pentecost. In later years, others looked upon those who had experienced the Azusa Street Revival with awe, respect, and honor.

The Azusa Street Revival began the modern Pentecostal movement with the emphasis on the tongues experience. Although many had spoken in tongues prior to 1906, these meetings brought attention to the world of the importance of the tongues phenomenon. Pentecostal leaders promoted the idea of sanctification as a "second work of grace" and simply added with the "Pentecostal baptism" the evidence of speaking in tongues as a "third blessing." [80]

Other Twentieth-Century Movements

Pentecostal and charismatic believers consider moves of the Spirit are associated with signs, wonders, healings, and miracles. Many persons belonging to the established denominations have had their own Pentecostal experiences. Many major denominations witnessed these movements. We have previously discussed these movements in the Methodist and Presbyterian churches, but others include the following.

1.   Catholic Charismatics. While some individual Catholics had been touched by the Pentecostal movement and had been baptized in the Spirit prior to 1967, the formation of a prayer group among faculty members and students at Duquesne University, Pittsburgh, in February 1967 is generally looked upon as the beginning of the charismatic renewal in the Catholic Church. [81]

2.   Episcopal Charismatics. Episcopal Renewal Ministries grew out of the Episcopal Charismatic Fellowship (ECF). That organization began in early 1973, when approximately three hundred Episcopal clergymen interested in charismatic renewal gathered at St. Matthew's Cathedral in Dallas, Texas. The meeting, a brainchild of the Reverend Dennis J. Bennett and the Reverend Wesley (Ted) Nelson, enabled participants to share the excitement generated by their common experience of the baptism with the Holy Spirit. Until that conference the extent of the outpouring of the Holy Spirit in the Episcopal Church was unknown. [82]

3.   Lutheran Charismatics. In the summer and fall of 1961 small groups of Lutherans in scattered locations in the U. S. began to have "charismatic experiences." The growth of the Lutheran charismatic movement in the U. S. during the 1960s was more widespread than most people realized. Even those involved in the movement were surprised when, with little publicity or fanfare, the first International Lutheran Conference on the Holy Spirit

drew more than nine thousand people to Minneapolis in 1972. This conference became an annual event and a focal point for renewal, with increasing attendance throughout the 1970s. [83]

4. Baptist Charismatics. The Pentecostal Free-Will Baptist church traces its Baptist roots to the eighteenth-century Baptist preacher Benjamin Randall. It organized in Dunn, North Carolina in 1908 as a Pentecostal church after G. B. Cashwell, who had himself experienced the Azusa Street Revival, led many Free-Will Baptists into a Pentecostal experience. Among Baptists nationally, fully 20 percent consider themselves Pentecostal or charismatic. The majority, however, has rejected charismatic practices, especially glossolalia. [84]

These are just a few examples of more current descriptions of charismatic awakenings. It is obvious that many in mainline denominations desire the strange phenomena associated with the Spirit. There must be a reckoning among all denominations that some believers will desire to move toward charismatic practices, while others may not. The church must respect both, and trust that moves of the Spirit will lead the church to its greater purpose.

So where will the church go from here? There is enough biblical and historical evidence that demonstrates the need for "freedom of the Spirit" and "respect for order and accountability." There is room for disagreements, tension, and struggle, but at the core should be an undeniable recognition of the preeminence of the Holy Spirit who governs and leads the church.

New Church and Holy Spirit

Dispensation of the Spirit

The dispensation of the Spirit is also the dispensation of the church. From historical trends, churches of mainline denominations have had moments of spiritual awakenings. For whatever the reason, structured orders of services have become more acceptable than worship practices representing freedom of the Spirit.

Historically, activities often associated with moves of the Spirit have confronted established beliefs and practices. If the church does not welcome the confrontation, then it assumes that the church has already obtained all truth and has already become all she is to be. It's obvious that the church does not make such claim. Therefore, the church should expect and welcome uncomfortable confrontation associated with moves of the Spirit as one way for addressing old structures, beliefs, and practices.

The church has not yet fulfilled God's plan and purpose for His church, and therefore things accomplished to this day are yet incomplete. There are things hidden and dormant waiting to be exposed. Even though we have seeds and small glimpses of how the church should be, the church has not yet realized her full potential. Therefore, we should learn from the past, but not be afraid of moving toward the future. The "not yet" aspect of the Kingdom beckons the church to come forth. Historically, this has not happened by smooth transition, but instead by conviction, confrontation, and conflict.

Emotional and Intellectual Displays of the Spirit

Emotion and intellect as well as faith and reason go together. There has been a constant swing of focus regarding the ways of the Spirit in the emotional and intellectual. These have corresponded in contrasting themes as "faith and reason," "miraculous evidence and scientific proof," "experience and explanation," "freedom and accountability," and "heretical or sound doctrine."

Paul the apostle embraced both faith and reason as important aspects of the gospel. In much of his writings, he used reason to explain how Jesus is the promised Messiah who has come. On other occasions he described the gospel as being foolishness to the Greeks and a stumbling block to the Jews. Simple faith in the cross of Christ evokes both, the power and wisdom of God. He says:

> For Jews request a sign, and Greeks seek after wisdom; but we preach Christ crucified, to the Jews a stumbling block and to the Greeks foolishness, but to those who are called, both Jews and Greeks, Christ the power of God and the wisdom of God. Because the foolishness of God is wiser than men, and the weakness of God is stronger than men.
> —1 Cor. 1:22-25

Some have often considered ways for expressing freedom of the Spirit as heretical because moves of the Spirit emphasized subjective inner convictions rather than outward objectivity and accountability. Historically, those who had different convictions than the established church did not desire to separate from the church, but in choosing between moving with their convictions or affirming the established views, they chose their convictions. It has been through these movements that beliefs, ideas, and practices have progressed toward diverse views of God working with humanity.

Spiritual Pursuits in Pentecostal Scholarship

Pentecostalism has often been associated with wild behavior applicable only to the unlearned. Academic circles have not readily accepted these expressions, being concerned that the Pentecostal experience does not pass scholastic rigor. For some, "Pentecostal scholarship" is an oxymoron, but there has been significant progress in education concerning the mysterious ways of the Spirit.

Since the early church, moves of the Spirit have been associated with the unlearned. Peter and John were uneducated men, but because of the powerful move of the Spirit in healing the lame man, many knew they had been with Jesus (see Acts 4:13, 14). Therefore, scholarship and Pentecostalism have not been close partners, but the acceptance of the spiritual has made and continues to make significant contributions in academia. For example, from the monastic period, Benedict of Nursia (AD 480-547), known for his disciplined desire for the spiritual, pursued literary achievements, as well. In addition, some major universities in America today have had in their foundations spiritual revivals and awakenings.

One would think that if something is birthed out of spiritual awakenings, then writings and discussions of the spiritual would be key components of its curriculum. However, in many theological schools of learning, curriculum concerning moves of the Holy Spirit is lacking.

As Clement of Alexander in the second century used the language of philosophical ideas to argue the credibility of Christianity and bring Christianity into societal acceptance, so will Pentecostalism use scholastic rigor to become more acceptable in academia. In a similar way (not necessarily like Clement of Alexandria who used rules governing philosophy), those who affirm the mysterious moves of the Spirit are communicating such phenomena in academic arenas and passing the test of scholastic rigor. Pentecostalism is no longer an enemy, but a true friend that stretches academia in ways that may be uncomfortable but is essential for moving the church forward.

Gordon Donald Fee (1934—) is one among many contemporary Pentecostal scholars who has defended Pentecostalism with theological and scholastic rigor. He has also received great respect among other theologians. Fee was conferred the Ph.D. degree in NT studies by the University of Southern California in 1966. Since 1986, he has been professor of NT at Regent College in Vancouver, British Columbia.

As a teacher, Fee is known for his contagious enthusiasm and passionate love for Scripture. He also has a reputation for insisting on conscientious and careful scholarship. A demanding teacher, he attracts students from a variety of traditions. He has convinced many that excellence in scholarship can be coupled with a deep devotion to God.

Within Pentecostal circles Fee is both admired and denounced. His careful regard for "scholastic tests" and his skills as a NT exegete renders him a voice to be reckoned. Also, his zeal behind the pulpit and his passion for the Pentecostal message of the Spirit's presence in this age authenticates him as one deeply committed to the Pentecostal experience.[85]

Yet, to others, Fee challenges the traditional Pentecostal hermeneutic doctrine that speaking in tongues is the initial physical evidence of Spirit baptism. In this, Fee becomes a threat to some Pentecostals.

Revivals, Outpourings, and Eschatology

> For it is impossible for those who were once enlightened, and have tasted the heavenly gift, and have become partakers of the Holy Spirit, and have tasted the good word of God and the powers of the age to come.
> —Heb. 6:4, 5

The reality of the "now is" and "not yet" of God's Kingdom creates a tension and expectancy that the church must live. The return of Christ is not only of a certain time in the future, but the essence of the promise has already come with the evidence of His Spirit (see 1 John 3:24; 1 John 4:13). The Spirit now works through the Christian community to bring about the completion of all things. Revivals, outpourings, and awakenings are essential for bringing the "not yet" into the realm of the "now is." Therefore revivals and outpourings are not just emotional touches. They are essential for transformation.

In the early church, the coming of the Spirit gave evidence of the heavenly gift having come as a "down payment" toward the full completion of more to come. Evidence of the Spirit gave witness to the resurrected Lord as a living presence among His church, and will soon return for His church. The tension of the "already" of the Kingdom with that of the "not yet" expectation of the promise, is a mysterious bond that moves the church forward.

The reality of the Spirit was so strong in the early church that many accepted the idea that the church had already entered the apocalyptic "last days" movement, and the glorified Lord would soon return. More than two thousand years later the church continues to wait. Until such time, the Holy Spirit is the foretaste of that which is to come.

Outpourings may be uncomfortable for some, but are essential for embracing the realm of the futuristic "not yet." Outpourings provide a greater awareness of the supernatural spiritual realm, bringing greater awareness of the futuristic and eternal into the realm of the present. Finding words to express the "not yet" is not easy, but by the Spirit, the church enters this realm in a moment. Like a pregnant woman, seeds of the "not yet" are already implanted within the hearts of believers, growing more and more until new birth of the church takes place.

Another Perspective Concerning Tongues

Concerning the problem of speaking in tongues with the Corinthian church there is another view worth considering (see 1 Cor. 14). The Corinthians thought that speaking in tongues was the best gift, the one that lifted them to a higher form of spirituality. The apostle Paul did not rebuke them nor discourage them from speaking in tongues, but emphasized the importance of maintaining order and edifying the church body.

The problem facing many worship gatherings in the church today is not of having too little order, but instead there is too much order and not enough edification. There is not a problem of too many speaking in tongues, but instead of not enough speaking in tongues. If the apostle Paul would visit our churches today he would probably wonder why there is so little of the spiritual, mysterious, and supernatural happening in our worship services.

The apostle Paul would probably encourage the church today to desire more of the spiritual and not be afraid of speaking in tongues (see 1 Cor. 14:1, 18, 39). He would welcome the church to cry out for more manifestations of the Spirit. He would encourage the church not to be afraid of losing control, and learn to yield to the leading of the Spirit.

This of course will lead to excesses, but will also give birth to something more of the spiritual the church desperately needs.

Conclusion

Views for greater acceptance of speaking in tongues does not mean one is more spiritual, but neither does it mean that one is of the devil. Simply stated; those who see its benefit will speak in tongues, while those who don't will not speak. There is a bigger picture that should move the church beyond its differences concerning tongues and gifts of the Spirit. It's the unity of the church.

There have been disagreements concerning moves of the Spirit within and beyond denominations. These will not go away, but there is a way for moving forward. Academia and mainline denominations have focused on the intellectual and shunned the emotional. On the other hand, the Pentecostal charismatic movement has highlighted the emotional and mysterious over the intellect and reason. It should prove fruitful among theological institutions and denominations to have discussions that include both as important ways of the Spirit. Discussion toward bringing together the two sides is no small order, but should prove fruitful for the church.

Discussions of the mysterious workings of the Holy Spirit are not just for Pentecostals, but are for the church. The church must pursue mysterious ways of the Spirit, and accept the fact that they are difficult to explain. Developing a model to address the dichotomy of individual convictions with those of established doctrine and tradition is a worthwhile endeavor. Where is the bridge for holding these together? It is unity of the Spirit.

Questions for Further Discussion

1. What are the church's fears of moving more toward the mysterious ways of the Spirit?

2. What might it require of church leaders to allow freedom of the Spirit?

3. What might be the reasons that many seek spiritual development but do not attend church, and neither do they look to the church for guidance?

4. What are key images and models for balancing freedom of the Spirit with submitting to the authority of church leadership?

CHAPTER FIVE

UNITY OF THE SPIRIT

...fellowship, in the breaking of bread, and in prayers...had all things in common, continuing daily with one accord...

—Acts 2:42, 46

Old Church Disunity

THE CHURCH IS more polarized concerning expressions of the Holy Spirit than about any other aspect of the church. Martin E. Marty, a professor of church history, makes the point that division in the church happens more because of preference of behaviors than differences in doctrine. [86]

We shall notice that church unity does not require the church to believe the same doctrines, traditions, and practices, but it does require "unity of the Spirit." These concepts will continue to have mysterious undertakings that will move the church toward becoming more aware of seeing through "eyes of the Spirit" how the Spirit binds believers together as one body of Christ.

This unity does not happen without great conflict and sacrifice. This does not mean that we forsake all of our ideas, but it will require forsaking or altering ideas that frustrate the answer to Jesus' prayer for church unity.

Therefore, important questions will arise such as these: How does this unity look? If the church will be one, how will it happen? What is the cost? To what degree are local churches, denominations, and church leaders willing to sacrifice for the sake of unity of the church?

These questions should cause the church to become more sensitive to the heart cry of unity from Jesus, "that they all may be one" (John 17:21).

103

Protestantism and Denominationalism

As previously stated, describing the church in North America is a complex issue. The most striking feature is the multiplicity of separate denominations and independent churches. American Protestantism contains many churches with membership as few as twenty-five, and denominations whose membership may be more than nine million. There are more Christian churches and denominations in America than in any other country.

Church diversity expressed in North America gives great challenge to a united church. Presbyterians, Lutherans, Baptists, Methodists, Pentecostals, and many others give expressions to various doctrines, traditions, and practices. Our American soil has provided ideal grounds for the proliferation of sectarian churches beyond anywhere and anytime in Christendom.

In a religiously pluralistic society where tolerance was necessary for political survival, North American Protestants tended to think of the church as an invisible reality consisting of all true believers, and denominations as voluntary organizations that believers create and join according to their convictions and preferences to represent the visible church.[87]

In the early American church experience, the idea of tolerance given to local communities allowed them to worship according to their particular values and traditions. Tolerance allowed for diverse ways of worship in the same community and was essential for the forming of this nation.

The discovery of America and the birth of Protestantism were almost contemporaneous events. For almost four centuries, this experiment of separation of church and state has allowed freedom of religious expression to spread throughout America.

In light of this freedom of diversity, a multitude of Christians are awakening to a spiritual poverty of their own denomination or church. They desire a greater richness of unity and fellowship. The church in North America is therefore in a unique position, not only geographically but also historically. The American church can further the movement of the Reformers of the sixteenth century and demonstrate the heartfelt prayer of Jesus, "that they all may be one." Let's notice how this unity was evident in the early church.

Early Church Unity

> Now the multitude of those who believed were of one heart and one
> soul;...they had all things in common.
>
> —Acts 4:32

The obvious question that arises is in what did the common bond,
deep ties, and ultimate foundation of unity among early believers in Christ
consist? The answer appears in the motives of having in common the
one God who has called all, one Lord Jesus Christ to whom all belong,
one Spirit who unites the one body of Christ, one baptism in which all
become "one in Christ Jesus" (see Gal. 3:27ff; 1 Cor. 12:13), and one
bread of the Eucharist in which all share (see 1 Cor. 10:17). Despite local
differences, ultimately what bonded early Christians together was the
common confession of their Lord, their common love for one another,
the common teachings of the apostles, and common eschatological
expectations of the Kingdom of God.

Unity of Fellowship

In the early church, committed relationship in the bond of fellowship
was essential for survival. Richard Niebuhr describes this need.

> When a first-century Jew or pagan decided to become a Christian, he
> became dependent upon a new community for the supplying of all
> his needs in a way which the modern Christian, at any rate within the
> West, can scarcely imagine. The church had to assume almost total
> responsibility for the whole person of its members and for every aspect
> of their relations with one another. [88]

The idea of "being together" appears throughout the early church to describe their regular fellowship. They gathered *together*. They suffered *together*.
They joined *together*. They prayed *together*. They assembled *together*. They
reasoned *together*. They took counsel *together*. They ate *together*. Therefore,
in the early church, many things happened while they were "together."

Separate and Different, but Community

The gospel spread to various communities during the early church.
Each community had particular distinctions from others. However,
there was a common bond that connected them together as Christian

communities. Distinctions did not nullify unity, but in some way enhanced it. However, on some occasions, differences produced sectarianism. The apostle Paul acknowledged this:

> For when one says, "I am of Paul," and another, "I am of Apollos," are you not carnal?....Therefore let no one boast in men. For all things are yours.
>
> —1 Cor. 3:4, 21

Acts chapter fifteen describes how the apostles worked through disagreements to identify how the church should allow differences as long they maintain important truths. James and the apostles agreed that the church would not require Gentile believers to worship with Jewish customs, but as long as Gentiles were sensitive to important truths, the church would allow them to worship and practice Christianity in their unique ways.

Was the unity described in Acts chapter two lost in chapter fifteen? Probably not. Unity is a complex idea to identify because it goes beyond uniformity or sameness to deeper levels of the Spirit where believers commit to one another. The early church was deliberate in promoting this unity, and apostolic leadership was decisive in leading the way. An essential component of unity was respecting differences while identifying and maintaining important truths.

A look at church history identifies seeds where the established church has blurred the idea of unity in one sense, but in another sense has provided opportunities for greater expressions of unity.

Historic Church Unity and Disunity

The task of searching and describing church unity in the light of its history is monumental, especially when models for unity are nebulous and unclear. How can one describe something if identifying it is unclear? A look at history can provide answers to what is not unity. However, describing what unity is becomes more challenging. In pursuit of greater unity, the church of today can avoid the pitfalls from its history.

The historic church did not handle conflicting personal convictions very well, and those with such convictions broke ties with the established institution of the church. While a form of unity existed in the established church, unity of the Spirit with freedom and diversity did not.

The One Universal Church

Ignatius is responsible for the first known use of the Greek word *katholikos*, meaning "universal," "complete," and "whole" to describe the church. It is from the word *katholikos* that the word *catholic* comes.

When Ignatius wrote the Letter to Smyrna, about 107 AD, he used the word *catholic* as if it was a word already in use to describe the church. This has led many scholars to conclude that the term *catholic church* with its ecclesial connotation may have already been in use as early as the last quarter of the first century.[89]

Eusebius of Caesarea (265-339 AD), known as the Father of Church History, also promoted the idea of church unity.

> For him, the peace and unity of the church were of prime importance.... The final draft of his *Church History* did not simply seek to retell the various events in the earlier life of the church. It was really an apology that sought to show that Christianity was the ultimate goal of human history, particularly as seen within the context of the Roman Empire.[90]

Eusebius became the ecclesiastical and spiritual voice of the Constantine era. Constantine's idea of the Imperial Church seemed to have consumed him. This idea of the Imperial Church saw riches and pomp as signs of divine favor. Eusebius described with great joy and pride the beautiful churches built during this era.

However, what evolved with these buildings was a liturgy to fit them. These developed into a form of clerical aristocracy, similar to the imperial aristocracy, and often far from the common people. The church imitated the empire, not only in its liturgy, but also in its social structure.

Constantine and the Imperial Church

One may consider the Imperial Church of Constantine as a model for church unity. It demonstrated a bond with church and state. Prior to the fourth century, the church was more of a spiritual movement, and not well organized. However, through organization and structure, Constantine with Eusebius brought Christianity into an acceptable place in society. A historic snapshot of a bond between church and state happened during this period of Constantine in Eastern Orthodox Christianity.

Constantine became emperor at the beginning of the fourth century and established Constantinople as the "New Rome." Constantine considered himself as the representative of God on earth and brought a sacred recognition to the state, thereby acknowledging Christianity as the state religion.

Prior to Constantine, around 300 AD, Christians endured great sufferings and persecutions, and the non-Christian world considered them ignorant and barbaric. Constantine, however, ordered an end to persecutions and placed Christians in positions of governmental leadership. He built the Imperial Church in the center of town, and practicing Christianity became not only acceptable but also politically and socially beneficial.

During the reign of Constantine, an established centralized church recognized with prestige and power came into being. Christianity found its place in politics and society in ways that were new to Christendom. By placing the church in the center of the city, the church and the state operated in a uniform way.

During the fourth century, great heresies arose in Christendom. As theological battles raged, Constantinople, next to Rome, emerged as the second most recognized religious expression for Christianity. Constantine rejected the idea of submitting to any bishop of the church and reserved the right to determine his own religious practices.

In accepting Christianity, he also accepted other pagan practices including the "unconquered sun god." Constantine blended beliefs and practices of the two into his Imperial Church. Many followed the official theology of the Imperial Church not because of Christian convictions, but because of its political and social benefits.

For those Christians who were a part of this established church, life seemed like heaven on earth. On the other hand, however, others questioned its faithfulness to the Christian witness. To them, the Imperial Church was a great apostate, having become too much like the world.

Christian worship in the Imperial Church greatly impacted the idea of the church of today. Prior to Constantine's Imperial Church, Christian worship had been relatively simple in private homes, but architectural structures were now built and set aside exclusively for worship. Choirs developed and gestures indicating respect became the norm, such as imperial protocol and the burning of incense. Officiating ministers dressed in luxurious garments.

The Imperial Church on the surface may have seemed a perfect model for church unity. However, what had become the official religion of the empire was a deliberate mixture of Christianity with paganism. While some enjoyed the prosperity and benefits of the Imperial Church, others wanted to protect their Christian convictions and fled to monasteries to live more secluded and simple lives.

An important concept worth noting concerning church unity during the Constantine era is the impact of unified political and religious forces. One may infer that an established central church sanctioned by political and religious leaders demonstrates a unified church. This concept would later influence the Reformers in pursuing civil authorities to endorse and protect their separation from Roman Catholicism.

Roman Catholic Church

The church in Rome emerged as a unifying force of political and social integration and accrued such political and material power that it became itself a state as well as a church. For more than a thousand years the Roman Catholic Church ruled some of the most important territories of Europe and asserted its spiritual dominance over all other rulers and peoples.

Through a network of alliances with other rulers that sought to assure their own political and material interests, the Roman church maintained its spiritual dominance. Kings and emperors received their crowns in recognition of papal authority. Bloody wars also marked the whole period, and the Roman church always had a stake in military affairs.

Unity associated with the Imperial Church with Constantine and the Roman Catholic Church though distinct, also sought a "form of unity" through a national church supported by ruling authorities throughout nations. Constantine as emperor of Constantinople established the Imperial Church in the east, while the Roman church sought to gain support from existing emperors in Western Europe and North Africa. Civil and church governments bridged for motivating others to conform and serve in fear and retribution.

Martin Luther and the Reformation

The Reformation movement arose about 1500 to address the troubled state of the Roman church. With widespread clerical abuse, loss of papal credibility, and an unrelenting insistence from Christian humanists demanding the church to change, seeds of reformation were in place. Luther never espoused a radical departure from the Roman church as the Anabaptists did, but instead wanted to reform it.

The Reformation itself was an ecumenical awakening. The Reformers were out to rescue the "true church" from the clutch of an alien regime which held the true church captive. The Reformers perceived that the true church was bound in what Luther called "Babylonian captivity." The Reformers sought to free the church from its bondage, held captive through the papacy and hierarchical system of priest, bishops, and archbishops.

Luther's ambition for two decades was the hope of bringing a sweeping reform to the Roman Catholic Church. Such reformation, he believed, would abolish the papacy with its established hierarchy, and reunite all believers with the existing church. The reformation he envisioned focused on returning to biblical authority with the preaching of justification by faith in Christ and the priesthood of the believer.

What Luther started as an attempt to reform, others moved toward more radicalism against the organized church. Others had taken Luther's message and practiced freedoms that radically resisted the Roman church. At first, Luther welcomed these changes, but later became concerned with their excesses. These were laymen declaring themselves as prophets, claiming they did not need the Scriptures because God spoke directly to them.

Thus Luther's earlier views, seemingly more radical, were tempered into a theological conservatism obtained because of his attitude toward the Anabaptists on one hand and his hope for bringing reform in Rome on the other. In Luther's later years, his middle ground steered toward union requiring a base on creedal theological ideas. However, instead of reforming the church, Martin Luther was excommunicated and the Protestant movement continued.

Reformation Movement on Many Fronts

After the Protestant Reformation, accompanied by the emergence of other strong national states, the political dominance of the papacy minimized, and its diminished spiritual power repudiated throughout many European countries.

By 1529, six German representatives embraced the name "Protestant." This "protesting" referred to the emperor's attempt to suppress Luther. Gradually the movement spread throughout Germany. The movement affected other areas: Zwingli in Switzerland, Thomas Cranmer in England; and John Calvin in France.

Calvinism became the most important expression of the Reformation, and by the middle of the century, Geneva replaced Wittenberg as the main center of the Protestant world. Calvinism became the driving force of the Reformation in the last half of the sixteenth century.

Leaders of the Reformation proposed plans for union by formulating a theological doctrine upon which all could agree. They assumed that doctrinal peculiarities belonging to each must be fully reconciled before union could take place. However, obtaining theological consensus was too wide for union to take place.[91]

All proposals for unity, whether they originated in Germany, Switzerland, or England, rested on a creedal basis. Thus the independent geographical units of the Reformation were, before the end of the sixteenth century, frozen into entrenched sectarian divisions—Lutheranism, Presbyterianism, and Anglicanism, all separated from one another, becoming the source for reproducing more Protestant sectarianism.

Anabaptists and Radical Reformers

The Anabaptists and Radical Reformers represent many Protestant churches in North America church history. Instead of seeking to reform the church like Luther, Zwingli, Calvin, and Cranmer; Anabaptism promoted the idea of "come-outism"—similar to the concept discussed in the previous chapter in the section on Pentecostalism. Those who desire to be the true church must "come out" of the established traditional church.

The Anabaptists appeared in the early part of the sixteenth century. They emphasized restitution rather than reformation. Along with other radicals, they wanted to abolish all practices, traditions, and ceremonies of the medieval church and build a new church on New Testament principles and practices. The majority of Anabaptists thought the true church was local, autonomous, and composed only of heartfelt believers, baptized after giving confession of faith in Jesus Christ.

Gradually mainstream Anabaptists gave rise to other movements. One, the Mennonites, was a Christian movement that had begun with Conrad Grebel, a disciple of Zwingli, but later derived its name from Menno Simmons. Other enduring expressions of the radical reformation evolved in the next century as Baptists and Quakers.

Luther, Calvin, Zwingli, and Cranmer and all the fathers of Protestantism were engaged in rescuing and restoring the hidden church. They saw the Roman Catholic Church and Eastern Orthodox Church as carrying within themselves a scandalous schism in the body of Christ.

However, in their attempt to rescue the hidden church, diverse expressions of many churches through Protestantism emerged and continued to frustrate the idea of church unity.

The Reformation forced nearly everyone to make a choice between the old and the new, significantly affecting the idea of individualism in European and Western civilizations. The modern, individualistic, pluralistic, and culturally fragmented Western world, for better or for worse, is largely the child of the tumultuous Reformation movement.

The Impact of Individualism upon the Reformation

Further study of individual free will, alongside ways to constrain its excesses is a monumental task for which the church should benefit. However, the findings should uncover important truths for addressing one of the greatest problems of church history. The idea for balancing a respect for individual freedom while maintaining accountability to others should unfold secrets for true church unity.

During the Dark Ages of the Roman Catholic Church and the Imperial Church (AD 400-1400), the institutional church dominated. After this emerged a rebirth of the importance of the individual in the Renaissance period with Erasmus, a significant figure leading the way in what is later termed *secular humanism*.

This humanistic promotion of individualism influenced Luther, and he debated for limiting the authority of the Pope. However, Luther's ideas of individual free will separated from those of Erasmus. Luther's ideas called for a sharp redefinition that divided the laity and clergy, but did not accept the humanist's idea that "each man is a priest to himself."

Individualism has vastly impacted Protestant Christianity, even to the point where the idea of community is vague and almost lost. Individualism is such an important aspect in American society that any ideology that desires mass support must also have a personal appeal for individual benefits. This historical trend is far from early Christianity.

Notice Suzanne de Dietrich's ideas of the impact of individualism upon the church.

> Nothing could be farther from the things of the apostolic church than the type of modern individualism that insists that "religion is a private affair," or a single compartment of life. This was the notion that, in the nineteenth century, led to autonomy in philosophy, economics, politics, art, and science. Ever since then man has constructed his world on

his own terms, and since this world is no longer in submission to any transcendent principle, and no longer has any universal foundation, it is faced with chaos. [92]

The idea of individualism has had positive and negative effects. A positive benefit of being "justified by faith" emphasized the importance of having a personal relationship with God. The Protestant movement has rightly captured the idea of personal faith, but its negative effect overextends individualism and makes personal faith a private affair, thus minimizing the importance of corporate accountability.

In North American Protestantism, freedom and individualism has promoted the idea of self-sufficiency and unconcern for cooperation and community. In spite of the impact of individualism in the mindset of American Protestants, some denominations have made deliberate attempts to move beyond separation toward ecumenism and unity.

The Ecumenical Movement

Etymologically speaking, the term *ecumenical* differs from *catholic* (with a small "c") because even though it expresses the idea of universality, it does not express the idea of unity in faith and order, as does *catholic*. The term *catholic* would have been perfectly suited for the movement, but the present and historical use of the term would have caused ambiguity and confusion in light of its usage in the Roman Catholic Church. Thus the term *ecumenical* served to better describe the Protestant movement for promoting a united church.

In its seeking to restore unity, the Ecumenical movement is an awakening to the problem of Protestantism. American Protestantism is not a protest against the established church, but against other Protestants. Similar to attacks against the Roman church, some claim that Protestantism and denominationalism hinder the true church from displaying church unity.

Since the beginning of the twentieth century, various denominations have merged. Northern and Southern branches of Methodist have merged to form the United Methodist Church. The Evangelical Synod of North America and the Reformed Church merged to form the United Evangelical Church. It is also worth noting that the Methodists, Presbyterians, and Congregationalists of Canada merged in 1925 to form the United Church of Canada. [93]

A number of other denominations have either merged or are in discussion of merging. Thus, an increased interest for unity and less sectarianism is evident throughout the church in North America.

These movements reflect that American Protestantism is becoming aware of its denominational decay. These movements also reflect a growing indifference among laity in denominational differences. While walls of separation are weakening, church leaders who fear relinquishing power and control still resist these movements with formidable force.

New Church Unity

Jesus' final conversation with His disciples clearly demonstrates His passionate desire for the church to be one (see John 17:20-26). How this oneness happens is unclear, but it does have implications of being a visible unity that the world recognizes. When those who believe in Christ unite as one, then the world will see Jesus through His Body, the church. This unity Jesus ratifies with His own blood is the subject of the Lord's final prayer, and probably His deepest desire.

The true church is one church. The term *church* (*ekklesia*) as used in the NT has a twofold meaning: the redeemed community of believers called out by and to Christ, in fellowship with other believers worldwide and of all times. Secondarily, *church* also refers to the local gathering of individual fellowships.

The term for church more often used today focuses on the second meaning to convey the idea of local assemblies and denominational fellowships. However, this concept undermines the importance of the one church as the redeemed community.

At the risk of splitting hairs with semantics, the church of Jesus Christ is already and forever will be *one true church*. We may have different fellowships with different traditions and practices, but these fellowships give witness to the one body of Christ.

If the church considers unity as one of the primary factors for moving the body of Christ forward, the church must be willing to sacrifice more denominational differences and individual preferences to promote this unity. No single denomination can dictate the model of a united church, but it can be found within the framework of an ecumenical concept with open-minded consideration and respect for differences.

One problem that frustrates the idea of unity is that the church today does not do enough of what the apostles did in Acts chapter fifteen—work through differences and disagreements for achieving greater goals. More often than not, Christians quietly separate from one another instead of moving beyond their differences. New fellowships begin with persons still holding onto improper attitudes toward those with whom they separated.

The Protestant Counterpart to Roman Church Hierarchy

The most radical charge the Reformers brought against the Roman Catholic Church was that it had divided the church into two separate parts—the hierarchical priesthood or *clergy*, and the people, or *laity*. The effect of the Roman system, claimed the Reformers, was degradation of the church, making irresponsible people of docile subjects and followers, instead of empowering the corporate body of the faithful to be responsible to Christ, the Head of the church.

Morrison identifies four comparisons that show the Protestant church still maintains this same Roman church structure:

1. The denomination, like the hierarchy, has usurped the organs and functions of the ecumenical church.
2. The denominational system, like the hierarchical system, is an alien, man-made structure superimposed upon the true church of Christ.
3. The multiple schisms in Protestantism which create an impassable cleavage between the denominations and the ecumenical church correspond to the internal schism existing in the Roman church which sets the hierarchy apart from the true church of Christ's people by an impassable cleavage.
4. The absolute independence and autonomy of the denomination in carrying out the mission of the church as if it represented the whole church and the whole gospel, is analogous to the exclusive and autonomous administration of the church's mission by the hierarchy with no participation of the laity in planning and projecting it.[94]

Like the Roman church that the Reformers criticized, the true church is still in a "Babylonian Captivity," but now with denominational systems. The unfinished Reformation seeks to bring freedom to the true church, and like the Reformers, the church today must also confront the religious system to reform Protestantism itself.

Is the Protestant Reformation a Hindrance to Church Unity?

Yes and no. The Reformation of the sixteenth century was in essence a movement, not intending to separate from the established church but to reform it. The Reformers saw the Roman church as an institution that hindered free expression of the true church. However, what began as a movement for releasing the true church gave rise to continuous separation of Christian groups from one another with no end in sight.

One view of the Reformation is that it was a movement that is yet unfinished today. The church today has opportunity for moving toward greater unity of the church, and building upon this incomplete work of Reformation. After more than five hundred years, the church has not moved very far toward this unity.

> The Reformers longed for unity. But the time was unready for it. Luther and Calvin and Zwingli and Cranmer, working under historical conditions unfavorable to the maximum fulfillment of their common hope, could only bequeath to us an unfinished Reformation. Ours is the challenging mission, in a fairer time, with the advantage of historical experience…to complete the labors of the great Reformers, that their faith, by our faithfulness, under God, might be made perfect. [95]

Since the Reformation, many denominations and churches have established. The condition of the church today is similar to what the Reformers of the sixteenth century faced. There is a need to remove or modify the religious structures of the church so the true church may be set free.

It is evident that accomplishing reform is no easy task. Attempts to unify the church have often brought more polarization, often leading to further separation and forming other fellowships or denominations. However, unless the church today radically confronts its own structures that hinder freedom and unity, it will remain within the Babylonian Captivity, leaving the "store of opportunity" wearing the same "old hat."

Is Unity of Doctrine Essential?

Considering the Reformers' points of theological disagreement, an important question is whether unity of doctrine, even if it could be attained, is necessary for church unity. We must be content to affirm that within the whole course of church history, especially in Protestant history, doctrines and creeds do not produce any permanence of unity.

Doctrines and creeds are valuable in identifying and distinguishing beliefs. They are good for establishing identity, but on occasion doctrines and creeds set boundaries against those who believe differently and thereby exclude other believers unnecessarily.

Even within the life span of individual believers, beliefs can change, and adherence to doctrine can hinder such change. How much more problematic it would be to seek unity only on the basis of creeds and doctrines.

The church should maintain foundational doctrine to build upon, but denominational doctrines often go beyond foundational truths to include many aspects for expressing the Christian faith. Doctrines in this case can overextend and become too restrictive, interfering with personal convictions and growth.

An example is Martin Luther's experience. Near the beginning of the Reformation, Luther's views were more liberal and radical. However, near the end of his life, his views became more conservative. Luther modified his earlier enthusiasm for the liberty of the believer and felt the necessity of creedal formulations as the bases of unity. The change was a reaction to the sectarian radicals that caused the Reformers great annoyance. Neither Luther, nor Zwingli, nor Calvin could tolerate the liberties of the Anabaptists.

In light of doctrine, Baptists have historically shunned the use of creeds. This is not to say that they have not valued doctrinal statements. But instead, they don't consider a creedal statement as binding upon the conscience of believers as the New Testament. A Baptist may agree or disagree with any creed. [96]

The strength of Baptists is that they have multiple local churches with local autonomy and easily seek fellowship with other churches beyond Baptist denominations. These churches are growing in number and gaining ground, despite the collective intensity with which the denomination as a whole magnifies its uniqueness. The Baptists provide a working framework for seeing unity beyond creed and doctrinal agreements.

Therefore, the church must not quickly dismiss those with personal convictions that do not fit within the framework of all theological doctrine and institutional acceptance. Like the Reformers who confronted Roman church doctrine, sometimes the church should reexamine its denominational doctrines to ensure they do not interfere with personal piety and fellowship.

What Hinders Unity?

Morrison identifies eight class lines that keep Christian members together and also keep them from other Christians: 1) socio-economic; 2) cultural; 3) aesthetic lines, where one denomination elevates form and beauty and another magnifies spontaneity; 4) historical traditions; 5) devotional worship, activism, and forms of pietism; 6) conservative, liberal, or heretical; 7) immigrant populations; and 8) race.[97]

There is a cultural ethos within each denomination that binds its members together but keeps them separate from other Christians. Denominations have become class sectarian churches, often remaining separate from those who do not share their particular affinities. Thus a complacent exclusiveness is stimulated within the fellowship.

Cultural affinities are not bad. Community forms with persons having things in common. However, cultural affinities should not take precedence over Christian unity. In this case, diverse cultures may blend together and thus develop a greater culture where love for Christ and one another take precedence.

Morrison describes possible ideas for moving forward.

It is unrealistic and unnecessary to assume that the natural and legitimate class distinctions which have long been nursed behind denominational walls would suddenly disappear in the united church.... It would not be incompatible with the ecumenical fellowship for our denominations ....

There is no value now enjoyed by the denomination which must be given up in response to the ecumenical appeal save only the false and unchristian value of its churchism. The churchism of the denomination must give way; it is in absolute conflict with the freedom that is in Christ. But every true and legitimate value now treasured in the fellowship of denomination will be conserved in the richer fellowship of the united church. And not only conserved, but enhanced and heightened.[98]

Morrison is quite pessimistic in his views of denominational churches taking part in evolving into a united church. The church can be appreciative of what denominations have accomplished. However, in moving toward new attitudes and paradigms, leaders should not merely serve their denominational interests, but transcend them, to serve the Kingdom of God.

One weakness of the common model of denominational churches is that too much attention is toward promoting the denominational church and not enough toward promoting the Kingdom of God. Centralized governance often seeks to maintain tight control and highlight the importance of submission rather than preparing the people of God to serve in the Kingdom of God.

A More Subtle Factor Against Unity

Something happened during the Reformation between Luther and Zwingli at Marburg in their attempt to unify. This experience provides insight into another factor that hinders church unity.

In an attempt to negotiate union between the two movements, Luther made a statement to Zwingli that's commonly misunderstood. Luther refused to "take the hand" of Zwingli, saying, "You are of another spirit than we."

Many believe this statement reflected a clear difference of biblical interpretation in regard to communion. However, their deadlock may not have been because of theological differences. Morrison describes something else happening:

> In the background of their theological discussion, there was a conflict of political interests which haunted the entire colloquy. Zwingli was at that time engaged in forming his Swiss Protestant cantons in a league with Austria against the Swiss Roman Catholic cantons. The union of German and Swiss Protestantism would greatly strengthen this project. But Luther was opposed to such a league. He saw it as rebellion against the emperor, upon whom he was at that moment working to bring religious unity into the empire by means of an ecumenical council which he hoped the emperor would call.[99]

Luther believed that only a council called by the emperor would motivate and protect its members from papal and Roman church pressure. Receiving the emperor's endorsement, Luther believed, would greatly enhance an ecumenical council free from papacy control.

Thus, there were two large forces hindering the union of the early Reformers of Luther, Zwingli, and Calvin. One may have been differences in creedal theological issues, but a greater hindrance seemed to be political factors—differences over gaining power through the cooperation of church and state.

If this observation concerning Luther is correct, then it should concern the church that sometimes differences are not from biblical interpretation but instead from political preferences and personal interests. Sometimes leaders in the church pursue and protect personal and political preferences at the expense of Christian unity.

Therefore, in further discussions for church unity, persons should be encouraged to make disclaimers of personal interests and bias. It's important to communicate personal preferences, political, social, and economic interests, and how these may interplay with accepting one another as true brothers and sisters in the body of Christ. When the cry of Christ for unity becomes the heartbeat of believers, then personal preferences and politics become secondary.

Individualism vs. Community

One of the major strengths of the church in America is emphasis on the individual. This is also its major weakness. There is an imbalance of the importance of individual and community in Western Christianity. Since the Renaissance and Protestant Reformation, the idea of individualism has developed to the point that many professing Christians see little or no need to affiliate with the local church. Many today use the Internet and television as ways for relating to other Christians. An isolated Christian is a far cry from the idea of the early church, but it's a reality that needs addressing in the church today.

All too often, many believers practice their faith as an "individual religion." This is a product of postindustrial society where religion has become a private affair that one can individualize and express in isolation. This may be America's majority faith expression, with institutional and communal faith being secondary.

Churches are losing as many members as they are gaining, not necessarily from the roll but by indifference and non-attendance. The reasons for this are numerous, but fundamentally, there is a lack of motivation for believers to serve in their churches and denominations.

While many Christians view serving in the church as a way for expressing their salvation, they fail to make the connection of serving in the Kingdom of God. This includes the idea that as individuals believe in Christ, they should become members of the "body of Christ," so connected with other believers that God's kingdom is better represented through believers with diverse races, cultures, backgrounds, and socioeconomic classes.

How can we attain a united church which welcomes and embraces our differences? What shall be the attitude of believers concerning these differences? According to Morrison:

> There can be only one answer. They must be welcomed and embraced as essential to the fulfillment of the Christian life. Our diversities are not a spiritual liability, but a spiritual asset, of the Christian life....Embraced in the ecumenical church, these diversities, freely intermingling and interacting, would stimulate, guide and enhance its spiritual life beyond anything we have now in our sectarian separation. [100]

All Are Yours

In the early church, the apostle Paul celebrated differences by saying they all belonged to everyone for the benefit of the body (see 1 Cor. 3:4-8). An overextended loyal commitment to a sectarian and denominational church, at the expense of Kingdom representation, shuts out the great treasures of spiritual unity available in other denominations.

Therefore, the treasures of Lutherans should not be only for the followers of Luther. The treasures of Presbyterians should not belong only to the followers of Calvin. Nor should the treasures of Anglicanism belong only to the followers of Cranmer. Nor those of Methodism belong only to the followers of Wesley. Nor does the move of the Holy Spirit belong only to the Pentecostals. Nor does any other tradition or revelation of Christ belong only to the denomination of those who celebrate them. What Paul the apostle said to the church at Corinth should also resound to the church of today: "All are yours." (see 1 Cor. 3:21, 22)

A united Protestant church, according to Morrison, must not be another denomination, but instead:

> It will be a church of the Christian people. In them, under Christ, will be vested the sole responsibility to determine its character and work. It will thus be a growing Church, not a static one. It will be, under Christ, a responsible Church, not dependent upon any priestly class. It will be a Church characterized by diversity, not by uniformity, for the Spirit is not manifested in uniformity, but in diversity. It will be a perennially reformable Church, for it will not always follow the Spirit's guidance and will never claim infallibility. It will be a fellowship within which each member attains, under Christ, the full freedom and the highest fulfillment of his personal life, not a 'docile multitude' of depersonalized

followers who have yielded their souls to the management of any self-constituted human authority. [101]

We can expect no spiritual awakening in Protestantism until the church set its hands and heart to the great task of giving back to Jesus Christ the church which sectarianism has robbed Him of—the church for whose life He died, and for whom He desires to see His prayer fulfilled, "that they all may be one."

Conclusion

It is naïve to think church unity happens peaceably. Unity will not happen in a peaceful and passive way where believers who think it to be a good idea will just pursue it. Instead, unity comes out of persecution and conflict. Those in fear of losing denominational identity and maintaining sectarian denominationalism will resist movements toward this unity.

Just as there was great conflict during the Reformation, we should expect conflict for any pursuits toward church unity today. However, a conviction for moving forward is a desire to develop a greater respect for all of Christ's body, the church.

An important question raised in the pursuit of unity is what distinguishes "true" and "false" Christianity? Are we one church regardless of beliefs and practices? The early and historic church had to address this, and so must the church of today. This is the topic of our next chapter.

Questions for Further Research and Discussion

1. What are some practical ideas that suggest how church unity looks?

2. What are the essentials for moving the church toward demonstrating this unity?

3. What are the elements of unity that already exist and are being overlooked?

4. What needs to happen for unity to happen among Jew and Gentile believers?

5. What are the costs and sacrifices the church needs to make for moving toward church unity?

6. To what degree might the idea of unity bring change to independent churches and denominations?

7. To what degree might local churches, denominations, and church leaders sacrifice for the sake of unity of the church?

CHAPTER SIX

JUDGING THE TRUE AND FALSE

"Be saved from this perverse generation."

—Acts 2:40

Old Church—True or False?

PROBLEMS FACING FALSE Christianity are as old as Christianity itself. Since the first century, the church has established criteria for distinguishing between true and false Christianity.[102] Convictions from subjective revelations of what a person or group of persons believe may often confront established views. However, there should be some criteria for examining these beliefs to determine if they represent true Christianity.

The church gives too little attention for examining and exposing aspects of Christianity that negatively impact the church. This requires addressing some difficult questions. Who determines the criteria for judging the true from the false? What parameters distinguish the true from the false? In what ways might the church declare these truths to churches and Christian communities? How does a believer or a group of believers freely practice their convictions when they differ from acceptable Christian doctrine, tradition, and practice?

A Disturbing Reality

Derek Prince points out a disturbing reality in the church today. He says:

Many of us come to church with needs. If we focus merely on our needs, we will never come to the end of them; rather, we will live with them forever. Something must release us from a myopic focus on our own needs, drawing us beyond the realm of "I need, I want, help me, pray for me, bless me." As long as we dwell on such things, we remain enslaved by them. We need to press past a self-centered focus to acquire the wisdom of God.

The ultimate purpose of everything is not related to us; it is related to God, who is both beginning and end. The world may not recognize this truth, but we, as Christians, do, and should reflect the centrality of God in the way we live.[103]

In a land of tolerance, "live and let live," churches in America are more prone to accept one another rather than humbly confront ideas that may bring reproach to Christ and His church. The "religious experience" of tolerance has left a greater impression in America than that of witch hunts and burning at the stake. The idea of authentic Christianity is threatened when messages that claim to be Christian do not represent the message and witness of the Kingdom of God.

This disturbing realty points to the need for addressing a concept of Christianity that pervades the church. Historically, attention has been given in defense of the faith with right doctrine, but not enough has been given toward right fellowship and respect for those who stretch the church to move toward reform and restoration. Discerning the true from the false is not easy, but the church must address the need to do so in its pursuit of transformation.

Religion and Christianity

The greatest threat to the kingdom of God is not the world, but religion. It is not a threat in the sense that it will overpower God's Kingdom. Instead, it is a threat in that religion deceives, distracts, and can divert sincere believers away from true worship. Religion looks like the Kingdom of God but does not bring change. Oftentimes religion entangles believers with the bondage of busyness and much church activity instead of serving with joy in the Kingdom.

The spirit of religion that Jesus confronted with the Scribes and Pharisees still operates in the church today. *Religion* is man's way of trying to connect with God. Christianity, on the other hand, is God's way of connecting with man. There is a vast but subtle difference between the two.

Mark Lawson asserts:

> The devil is not fighting religion; he is too smart for that. He is producing a counterfeit Christianity so much like the real one that good Christians are afraid to speak out against it....We are plainly told in the Scriptures that in the last days men will not endure sound doctrine and will depart from the truth and heap to themselves teachers to tickle their ears. We live in an epidemic of this itch, and popular preachers have developed ear tickling to a fine art. Today, the angle is to avoid "negative" preaching and accentuate only the positive.[104]

The goal of a religious system is primarily to get people in and make it hard for them to get out. Whether persons find spiritual nurturing or not, the religious system is more interested in maintaining control rather than setting people free with the grace of God.

Religious leadership is therefore a false type of leadership that becomes a hindrance to promoting God's Kingdom and government. Church leaders ensnared with religious controls may not be aware of it. Identifying religious deception and false leadership is difficult because it looks genuine.

Christless Christianity

Michael Horton describes a condition of Christianity in America in his book *Christless Christianity, The Alternative Gospel of the American Church*. In his attempt to raise critical issues addressing the church today, some of his concerns are well founded, while others lack support.

Horton is correct in claiming that too many messages commonly preached in American churches focus on the individual rather than on Christ. He offers this opinion:

> Despite significant differences across these generations and types of church ministry, crucial similarities remain. The focus still seems to be on us and our activity rather than on God and his work in Jesus Christ....Besides the preaching, our practices reveal that we are focused on ourselves and our activity more than on God and his saving work among us...the "search for the sacred" in America is largely oriented to what happens inside of us, in our own personal experience, than in what God has done for us in history.[105]

However, Horton wrongly minimizes the importance of personal conviction in the believer's life. Horton does not distinguish between *privatized* experience and *personal* experience. He uses them interchangeably, but there are significant differences and understanding these distinctions is critical for moving forward.

In citing Max Weber's secularization theory, Horton says;

First, religion is privatized, its domain shrunk to the island of private subjectivity. Statements such as "Jesus is alive" and "Jesus is Lord" are no longer regarded as objective, public claims based on historical events but become references to one's personal experience....Once privatized, religion becomes *relativized*. No longer *truth*, it is *your* truth. Since religious beliefs are no longer claims about public events, they can only be justified now in terms of what each individual finds meaningful, useful, and transformative.[106]

Horton's position on personal experience has caused concern throughout Christendom. Oftentimes the church has considered these subjective ideas heretical. However, subjective experiences are not necessarily "privatized experiences" as Horton describes. Unlike a privatized faith, personal convictions include the individual but also belong to the community for scrutiny and accountability.

Personal conviction can be like Luther's convictions on justification by faith and the priesthood of believers. These were personal but also belonged to the church community. Even Luther welcomed these for discussion and reform.

Horton's position promotes the same idea of what drove many from the established, organized church during the Reformation. He says; "If Christianity is about public truth delivered through an external Word, then ministry and evangelism require educated leaders who can expound and apply that truth for the benefit of those under their care."[107] This is the same idea the Reformers antagonized.

Horton's position remains within an ideological framework that fails to accept the importance of many believers who desire to experience God in ways that do not easily fit within acceptable intellectual and ritualistic religious frameworks.

It is not my intention to refute Horton's attempt to raise a critical problem in the church, but instead to note that the concern he names as "our captivity"[108] does not adequately address the issue. Institutional church rituals do not satisfy many who desire a more personal experience. These desires are more personal and subjective as evident in Monasticism, the Reformers, and many Protestants today. Personal and subjective faith is a vital part of Christianity that Horton seems to deny.

The Moravians, a spinoff from the Lutherans, promoted a more personal and spiritual faith. Pietism of the Moravians influenced Wesley, who later gave testimony of being raised in the church but lacking a personal saving faith. The Quakers opposed the natural reasoning of the Deists and desired personal encounters with the divine. The list can go on and on showing the importance of desires for personal faith and experience in the church. The accomplishments of these personal convictions throughout history cannot be dismissed and many continue to flee the organized church for a more personal spiritual experience.

Even though the heretical has also been associated with the subjective and personal, naming all as heretical is insufficient in identifying and solving the problem. Seeking ways to distinguish the true from the false is a worthy task and must continue, but every person who has personal convictions which conflict with established views is not necessarily heretical. If Horton's attempt at naming our captivity is insufficient, then what should be our criteria? Let's first lay foundation by taking a look at the early church.

Early Church—True or False?

Jesus Confronted Religion and False Leadership

> Woe to you, scribes and Pharisees, hypocrites! For you travel land and sea to win one proselyte, and when he is won, you make him twice as much a son of hell as yourselves.
>
> —Matt. 23:15

> Woe to you, scribes and Pharisees, hypocrites! For you cleanse the outside of the cup and dish, but inside they are full of extortion and self-indulgence.
>
> —Matt. 23:25

> Woe to you, scribes and Pharisees, hypocrites! For you are like whitewashed tombs which indeed appear beautiful outwardly, but inside are full of dead men's bones and all uncleanness. Even so you

also outwardly appear righteous to men, but inside you are full of hypocrisy and lawlessness.

—Matt. 23:27, 28

During his ministry, Jesus confronted Scribes and Pharisees, because on the surface they had an appearance of devotion and piety, but this did not reflect the condition of their hearts. On two occasions Jesus angrily entered the temple because the temple was used for personal profit rather than spiritual edification (John 2:15; Luke 19:45). The temple should have been the place where people could find hope, rest, and restoration with God, but instead, it became a place of profiteering, manipulation, and control.

The Scribes and Pharisees had a religious system that required those who desired to offer sacrifices to purchase doves and animals from the temple. Being able to sell sacrificial offerings at top price, the temple became a place for religious profiteering instead of prayer and worship. Jesus condemned such practices, saying, "… It is written, 'My house shall be called a house of prayer, but you have made it a den of thieves'" (Matt. 21:13).

Early Apostles Warn of False Leadership

For such are false apostles, deceitful workers, transforming themselves into the apostles of Christ. And no wonder! For Satan himself transforms himself into an angel of light.

—2 Cor. 11:13, 14

But there were also false prophets among the people, even as there will be false teachers among you, who will secretly bring in destructive heresies, even denying the Lord who bought them, and bring on themselves swift destruction. And many will follow their destructive ways, because of whom the way of truth will be blasphemed. By covetousness they will exploit you with deceptive words.

—2 Pet. 2:1-3a

Throughout the early church, freedom was allowed as long as foundational truths were maintained. When such teachings or practices threatened doctrinal truths, apostolic authority took the lead in distinguishing between the true and the false.

Not only were there warnings of false leaders, the apostles warned against the spirit of the world finding its way in the life of the church.

> Beloved, do not believe every spirit, but test the spirits, whether they are
> of God; because many false prophets have gone out into the world....
> They are of the world. Therefore they speak as of the world, and the
> world hears them.
>
> —1 John 4:1, 5

When adherence to sound doctrine is absent, persons succumb to
what the Bible calls "strong delusion." This happens because they did
not receive the truth.

> And for this reason God will send them strong delusion, that they should
> believe the lie, that they all may be condemned who did not believe the
> truth, but had pleasure in unrighteousness.
>
> —2 Thess. 2:11-12

Since the early church warned of the false, shouldn't the church of
today do likewise? Many Christians become victims to a deceptive religious
spirit, having "a form of godliness, but denying its power" (2 Tim. 3:5).

Historic Church—True or False?

Apologetics and Heretical Conflicts

As previously stated, second century Christianity did not have
the luxury of ready acceptance by the masses. Instead, many accused
Christians of being uncultured barbarians. They considered Christians
barbaric because they were rooted in Jewish antiquities and not in Greek
or Roman ideologies.

In attempts to argue the strength of Christian teachings, historic church
leaders sought to communicate Christianity within the context of acceptable classical literature of the period. Thus, on one hand, it was necessary
to separate Christianity from false teachings, but on the other, there was
an attempt to present Christian concepts in ways acceptable to society.

The term heresy (hairesis) in the Greek refers to a philosophical school
or teaching in a Christian context to bring divisions and threaten unity
of the church (see 1 Cor. 11:19; Gal. 5:29; cf. Titus 3:10). The problem
of heresy as it was to be later defined, over against orthodoxy, refers to
false teachers who "bring in destructive heresies" in the denial of Christ.
The letters of Paul and John warn the Christian church to resist doctrinal
error within its ranks. [109]

To distinguish true Christianity from heretical teachings, the church established creeds and canons. Creeds were significant for solidifying concepts of "the one true catholic (universal) church." Therefore, through approval of writings canonized into the New Testament and establishing doctrinal creeds, the early historic church sought to crystallize Christian thought and distinguish it from heretical teachings.

The Apostles' Creed

The Apostles' Creed, written around 150 AD, confronted Gnostic teachings. The Creed affirmed the essence of Jesus. It affirmed that Jesus is the Son of God, conceived of a virgin, that He led a sinless life, died an atoning death, was buried and raised again from the dead three days later, and He will come again in power and glory to judge the living and the dead alike.

The Nicene Creed

In writing the Nicene Creed of 325 AD, church leaders responded to the Arian controversy. Arius taught, "If the Father begat the son, he that was begotten had a beginning of existence: and from this it is evident, that there was (a time) when the Son was not." Crucial to the question are the doctrines of creation and the Trinity. At Nicea, Christians adopted the teaching that the one Lord Jesus Christ from eternity is of one substance with the Father.[110]

Athanasius concerned his argument with the formula "of a similar substance." Describing the essence of Jesus, he declared that it was acceptable to refer to the Father, Son, and Holy Spirit as "one substance" as long as it did not dismiss the distinction among the Three as the Trinity. On the basis of this argument, most of the church rallied to support the Council of Nicea. The church eventually ratified this doctrine, at the Second Ecumenical Council in Constantinople in 381 AD.

The Nicene Creed crystallized important truths of Christian doctrine that continue as basic tenets of the Christian faith.

The Canon of the New Testament

In the second century various writings circulated claiming to present the true teachings of Jesus. In response to these writings, the church sought to base accepted doctrines on the consensus of the entire apostolic tradition. The writings included in the New Testament as we have it today were accepted and compiled as *Canon*, meaning "to have passed the test of integrity and credibility."

Although the Canon of the New Testament and the Creeds were valuable instruments for addressing heresies, the debate also addressed the issue of the authority of the church.

This was important, not only because someone had to decide who was right and who was wrong, but because of the very nature of the issue of authority being at stake. All agreed that the true message was the one taught by Jesus. However, who were the ones that should interpret that message? Thus, the debate of validating acceptable writings was also an issue of church authority who could make claims against those considered heretics.

Let's observe a variety of those teachings, some that the church identified as acceptable and others it designated as heretical.

Gnosticism

The Gnostics claimed they had secret access to the original message through a succession of secret teachings. The term *Gnosticism* designates a variety of religious movements in the early centuries of Christianity that stressed salvation through secret knowledge (*gnosis*). Church leaders of the second century deemed these teachings as heretical perversions of Christianity.

Many Christians from the first and second centuries were of Greek background and had a hard time believing that Jesus was both divine and human because in Platonic thought the spirit was all-important, and the body was a prison from which one desired to escape. This trend of thought developed into teachings of Gnosticism.

Gnostics held that all physical matter was evil, the spiritual was good, and only the intellectual who were enlightened with "secret" knowledge could enjoy the benefits of spiritual freedom. It was difficult for Gnostics to accept the fact that Jesus was without sin, if he had a physical body. According to Gnosticism, the body itself was evil. Gnostics therefore taught that Jesus was actually a spirit who only appeared to have a body.

The apostle John confronted ideas of Gnosticism:

> Beloved, do not believe every spirit, but test the spirits, whether they are of God; because many false prophets have gone out into the world. By this you know the Spirit of God: Every spirit that confesses that

Jesus Christ has come in the flesh is of God, and every spirit that does not confess that Jesus Christ has come in the flesh is not of God. And this is the spirit of the Antichrist, which you have heard was coming, and is now already in the world.

—1 John 4:1-3

Marcion (About 144 AD)

Marcion posed an even greater threat to the church than did the Gnostics. Like them, he rejected or radically reinterpreted the doctrines of creation, incarnation, and resurrection. But he went beyond them in that he organized a "church" with bishops and established its own scripture. For a number of years, this rival so-called church achieved a measure of success, and even after it was clearly defeated it lingered on for centuries.

Marcion was convinced that the world was evil and concluded that its creator must be either evil or ignorant. According to Marcion, the God and Father of Jesus is not the same as Jehovah God of the Old Testament. It was Jehovah who made this world, and either through ignorance or out of an evil intent, made this physical world and placed humanity in it.

Montanism (About 150 AD)

Montanism takes its name from its founder, Montanus, who was a pagan priest until his conversion to Christianity in AD 155. He later began prophesying, declaring that he had been possessed by the Holy Spirit. Soon women also began prophesying. This in itself was not new, for at that time, at least in some churches, women prophesied. What was new, and gave rise to serious misgivings, was that Montanus and his followers claimed their movement was the beginning of a new age. This new age demanded believers to have a rigorous moral life, just as the Sermon on the Mount was more demanding than the Laws of the Old Testament. [111]

Montanism was a movement of believers that saw themselves as the elite of spiritual Christians who prepared themselves to be the "fit" bride for the coming Christ. The movement was a protest against growing formalism and worldliness in the established church. This movement bears resemblance to many sects that later birthed during the Reformation period.

Shortly after the middle of the second century Montanus proclaimed the imminent return of Christ with a new outpouring of the Holy Spirit as its sign. Preparation for the new advent was to be a withdrawal from the world. He called for special fast-days, and persecution was to be expected and even encouraged, so that the church would be a purified and fit bride for the coming Christ.

Opposition to Montanism came from Pope Eleutherus. By 230, he excommunicated the group, declaring them to be heretical. However, the movement continued underground, chiefly as a protest against growing worldliness and ritualistic formalism of the church. Tertullian, who later laid important groundwork for the Doctrine of the Trinity as a response to Marcion's teachings, was a notable product of Montanism.

Tertullian (160 - 215/20 AD)

Tertullian was not heretical, but in the second century he spoke against the idea of trying to blend Christianity with pagan philosophical ideas. His position was in contrast to Clement of Alexandria, who sought to blend Christianity with philosophical ideas.

Neither was Clement heretical, but the two held opposite sides of the issue concerning using philosophical ideas to explain Christianity. Tertullian summarized his position in a famous phrase: "What does Athens have to do with Jerusalem? What does the Academy have to do with the church?"[112]

Tertullian's conviction was that many heretical teachings that circulated during that period were the result of mixing pagan philosophies with Christian doctrine. If Christianity was to remain distinct from the world he felt it must rid itself of philosophical ideas that were not of the church.

Justin Martyr (100-165 AD)

Justin Martyr was significant in finding ways to bridge the divide between Christianity and classical ideologies of the day. In addressing this, Justin Martyr claimed that the philosophers were only correct by mere coincidence. Their methods and outcomes were mere glimpses of truth and not considered as conclusions of truth.

How, then, did Justin Martyr explain the partial agreement between the philosophers and Christianity? For him, the answer is in the doctrine of *the Logos*. This word in the Greek means both "word" and "reason." In his First Apology (152 AD), Justin argued that the teaching of Christ is older than all other writings. He asserts that the divine Logos had been in the world from the beginning, and the whole Logos resided in Jesus Christ.

Christianity was therefore the full revelation of truth because Christ was Himself the incarnation of the whole divine Logos.

What Justin did was to open the way for Christianity to claim its place with classical literature. Following Justin's inspiration, there were other Christians who tried to build further bridges between their faith and ancient classical literature.

Augustine, Manicheism, and Pelagianism

In his earlier years, Augustine followed the teachings of Mani, but there were doubts. Manicheism seemed to address Augustine's struggle with the origin of evil concerning freedom of the will and predestination. According the teachings of Manicheism:

> ...the human predicament is the presence in each of us of two principles. One, which he calls "light," is spiritual. The other, "darkness," is matter. Throughout the universe there are these two principles, both eternal: light and darkness.... The two have mingled, and the present human condition is the result of that admixture. Salvation then consists in separating the two elements, and in preparing our spirit for its return to the realm of pure light, in which it will be absorbed....According to Mani, this doctrine had been revealed in various fashions to a long series of prophets, including Buddha, Zoroaster, Jesus, and Mani himself. [113]

Later Augustine refuted the Manichees. Since he had led some friends to the religion, he felt some responsibility to refute the teachings he had earlier supported. Of particular importance was the Manichees' position on man's free will. They held that everything was predetermined and that humans had no freedom of will. Augustine, on the other hand, became a champion proponent of freedom of the will.

Pelagius agreed with Augustine that there is freedom of the will, and that the source of evil is in the will. As Pelagius taught it, this meant that human beings always have the ability to overcome sin.

Pelagianism, named after Pelagius, was an ascetic movement with distinctive theological positions that the church declared heretical. Pelagianism rejected the idea of original sin, and therefore, undermined the importance of atonement for sin through Jesus Christ. Pelagius claimed that each person comes to the world with complete freedom to sin, or not to sin. Children do not sin until they, on their own free will, decide to sin. [114]

Augustine's most important theological work came out against the teachings of Pelagius.

Gonzalez writes;

> According to Augustine, the power of sin is such that it takes hold of our will, and as long as we are under its sway we cannot move our will to be rid of it. The most we can accomplish is that struggle between willing and not willing, which does little more than show the powerlessness of our will against itself. The sinner can will nothing but sin. [115]

A comparison of these three teachings raises the awareness that a search for clarity of truth is an ongoing process and heresy is not easily recognizable. Much of Augustine's theology the church has accepted. While the church has rejected Manicheism and Pelagianism, both had influence on Augustine's struggle for clarity of truth.

Reformers or Roman Catholics

Which group is the heretic? Just as the established church declared the Reformers as heretical, the Reformers declared the Roman church as the "Babylonian Captivity," holding the true church in bondage. The Roman church simply excommunicated those who opposed them. Since the Reformers could not excommunicate the Roman church, the Reformers sought support and protection from governmental and secular authorities.

In the fifteenth century there was considerable discussion among Protestant and Catholic polemicists as to how to identify the true church. They developed a list, but Luther expanded this list to include seven essentials:

1. The preaching of the true word of God.
2. The proper administration of baptism.
3. The correct form of the Lord's Supper.
4. The power of the keys.
5. The lawful vocation and ordination of ministers.
6. Prayer and the singing of psalms in the vernacular.
7. Persecutions. [116]

We have noted the ongoing tensions of various persons or groups seeking to promote their particular teachings while refuting those of others. In doing so, the issue was not necessarily that teachings were false, but simply that persons went against the established teachings and practices of the church. One such case is that of John Wycliffe.

John Wycliffe, a Heretic? (1329-1384)

The ongoing challenge in distinguishing the true and false has consisted of two questions: Who is the authority that decides what is acceptable, and what are the criteria for proper judgment? Historically, the Roman church declared persons as heretics simply because they disagreed with church doctrine and practices. John Wycliffe, an English reformer, is a good example of how authority and judgment become questionable.

During the fourteenth century, the state of the church, being weak through a conflict of legitimacy of papacy, with two existing popes and corrupt practices of simony and nepotism, gave rise to various movements. John Wycliffe was the center of one such movement. He not only challenged the practices of the church, but also claimed that the church should reform its doctrines.

English authorities welcomed Wycliffe's arguments on the nature of authority and lordship. According to Wycliffe, all legitimate authority comes from God. However, such authority is characterized by the example of Christ, who came to serve, not to be served. Any authority used as lordship over others for profit is not true authority, but usurpation.

Wycliffe's assertions concerning authority brought friction. Considering the views of the church during that period, his position grew more radical as he taught that the true church is not the pope and his established hierarchy but rather the invisible body of those who are predestined for salvation. He drew this point from St. Augustine of Hippo. Toward the end of his life, Wycliffe declared that the pope is probably among those who were reprobate.

Wycliffe was a prolific writer who translated the Vulgate Bible into English. His belief was that the Bible was the only authoritative guide for faith and practice. In this light, Wycliffe's teachings were forerunners to the Protestant Reformation.

When Wycliffe died of a stroke in 1384, he was in communion with the church and buried in consecrated ground. However, in 1428, the Council of Constance later condemned him. His remains were exhumed and burned and the ashes thrown in the Swift River.

As we consider church history, finding consensus to distinguish the true from the false has been and will continue to be an ongoing challenge. However, it's a discussion worth pursuing. Wycliffe was one considered heretical, but he made great contributions to the church. If Wycliffe is a heretic, what does this say about Martin Luther, the Reformers, and many others rejected by the church whose ideas have greatly benefited the church? What might this say about the church's reluctance to accept hidden truth when these same truths, for others, have become beneficial and liberating?

In moving beyond our historical past for addressing these issues, we should explore ways to have serious yet humble discussions on ways to maintain accepted established truths while pursuing controversial hidden truths.

New Church—True or False?

Why Be Concerned?

…"Take heed that no one deceives you, For many will come in My name, saying, 'I am the Christ,' and will deceive many."

—Matt. 24:4,5

"Then many false prophets will rise up and deceive many. And because lawlessness will abound, the love of many will grow cold."

—Matt. 24:11,12

In a land of tolerance, judging error is minimal. Some issues concerning truth find discussion in the academic arena and some Christian magazines sound an alarm; however, there is still a lack of apostolic authority that speaks against church doctrines and practices that are either marginal or heretical.

Jesus warned His followers of false leaders and made a distinction by contrasting the ways of the Kingdom with the ways of the Scribes and Pharisees. Paul the apostle made a distinction between Christianity and Judaism. Acts chapter fifteen tells of a council among the apostles and church elders seeking to determine appropriate requirements for Gentile believers. John the apostle wrote his letters to make a distinction between Christianity and Gnosticism. Thus, the early church warned against those teachings that were distinct from Christianity.

The spirit of the world is not just a power working outside the church. The church has the calling to be in the world and not of the world (see John 17:15-16), with all the tensions and persecutions this entails. These distinctions are not by denominations or local assemblies but instead by

the degree of the spirit of the world that has become embedded in the
life of the church.

Judgment Begins in the House of God

> The time will come for judgment to begin at the house of God; and if
> it begins with us first, what will be the end of those who do not obey
> the gospel of God?
>
> —1 Pet. 4:17

One of the great themes of the end-time battles involves the church's
ability to judge lawlessness and unrighteousness. Until the church
improves its ability to clearly address the sins of the church, it will
continue being ineffective in judging unrighteousness in the world.

Many expect the Antichrist to come in the form of a political and
religious leader who will harness the collaboration of many for economic
prosperity. However, the spirit of antichrist is already at work, and the
church does not seem to recognize nor know how to address it.

Identifying and communicating truths that confront error is no easy
task. Even beyond the challenges of humble dialogue on critical issues
is also the impact of mass media and information. In today's generation,
believers and nonbelievers have access to various media through the
Internet and social networks, television, and so on. These make it very
difficult to address the many ideas released as teachings of the church.
Except that the church becomes engaged in such networks, the church
seems ineffective in its ability to exercise its authority.

Effective tools for addressing critical issues may continue to be found
in these media, as well as in Christian magazines and periodicals, books,
and discussions in the academic arena, wherever church leaders may raise
and discuss critical issues. In addition to these, identifying distinctions
must also be in the pulpits to prepare the body of believers to effectively
discern truth from error. Denominational platforms can more easily
communicate these distinctions to their constituents, but they should
do so in a spirit of respect and humility.

Naming Our Captivity

Michael Horton's *Christless Christianity* correctly holds that
Pelagianism is one of the major ideologies against the cross of Christ that
should concern the church today. However, his idea of "semi-Pelagianism"
does not have support in Pelagianism's concept of sin and free-will. [117]

Horton identifies *semi-Pelagianism* as the "process of salvation." His position does not acknowledge the continuous workings of salvation in the life of the individual. He does not include in his position that one may believe in the concept of original sin with the atonement of Christ, and also acknowledge that this work continues in the believer's life toward growth and maturity.

The legal aspect of salvation in the atonement of Christ is complete and does not require man's participation. However, the vital aspect of Christ's atonement does require man's participation in a continuous yielding and pursuing "in the process of salvation." Paul the apostle describes this as his main Christian objective:

> Brethren, I do not count myself to have apprehended; but one thing I do, forgetting those things which are behind and reaching forward to those things which are ahead, I press toward the goal of the prize of the upward call of God in Christ Jesus.
>
> —Phil. 3:13, 14

This idea of salvation that recognizes the process is important even though some, such as Horton, consider this concept to be heretical. Salvation which has a foundation in the redemptive work of Christ, but acknowledges the believer's continued growth in pursuing Christ challenges traditional concepts of Christianity. There has been and will continue to be believers who search for more ways of knowing Christ beyond what has commonly been accepted. They pursue additional ways for knowing Christ. Acknowledging the process of salvation (both individually and collectively) provides ample space for this movement and growth.

On the other hand, a static idea of salvation defined with an objective standard for Christianity is too restrictive for those who desire to pursue knowing Christ more personally. This requires recognizing the importance of subjective qualities that are hard to measure. These points are significant as we move toward "naming the captivity" that threatens true Christianity.

Pick the Right Fight

It's important to pick the right fight. Conservatives and liberals have often fought, with conservatives probably throwing the most punches. The Fundamentalists have gained the reputation for being great fighters for their definition of truth. Their hands are calloused from beating on the liberals. These fights are just as evident among local assemblies where congregations pay more attention to fighting their brothers and sisters than representing Christ. Instead of these, a better fight should be the church's concern about its representation of Christ to the community around.

Since the Christian faith is concerned with saving a lost world, believers are obligated to stand up for the truth and to contend for the faith when necessary. However, there is a better way than being overly concerned with dealing with those liberals in faith and theology. All believers can do more by just being Christlike and representing to the world that the church is truly the body of Christ and the family of God.

It is important for the church to recognize that how we relate to each other is our witness to the world. Conservatives and liberals, Episcopalians, Lutherans, Presbyterians, Baptist, Pentecostals, and all other sectarian fellowships that claim to represent Christ should begin with this important premise: The church is not a perfect church, but the church preparing to live together for eternity.

No one Christian group has a monopoly on truth. It is not merely our bold claims of what we believe is truth, but just as important is our humble submission of not knowing the whole truth. Not only do arguments concerning doctrine divide the church, but pride and arrogance do also. There is plenty of room for the whole church to repent. In our humble pursuit of truth, we should seek to represent Jesus Christ, who is the Truth, and thereby we call Him Lord.

Fight with Respect and Humility

There is biblical foundation for "excommunicating" one from the church. This purpose is not only for restoring the person, but also for sending a message to the rest of the body. However, excommunication is an ineffective tool for American Protestantism because if the church excommunicates someone that person may simply find fellowship elsewhere or start another church. A spirit of pride becomes evident when one is not open for correction. The spirit of pride can be present even when an error of doctrine is not.

The church must not only address incorrect doctrine but also address the spirit of pride that continues to work in the church. The spirit of pride is as great an enemy to the church as any other. Pride diminishes the importance of how much the church needs every member, even when the ideas of others are uncomfortable. The proud person does not admit any wrongs within himself nor give any allowance for others to change and grow.

Martin Luther demonstrated a spirit of humility, even though he disagreed with Roman church doctrine and practice. He shunned division and wanted to remain in and reform the church. He did all he could to remain connected. However, the Roman church was unprepared for his convictions. When they demanded that he recant, Luther refused. From that time forward, division was inevitable.

Luther's humility was evident not only in his ability to affirm his convictions but in his desire to remain connected and bring change in the church. Luther's willingness to change was evident in his later years. He took positions that were less radical and more favorable to mending what had previously been torn away.

Looking through a Dark Glass

The church has a twofold nature. Through the Spirit it shares in God's life; but also made up of human stuff, it must deal with sinful men with the lures of this present world. This mystery of the incarnation continues in the church, and we live with the tension of the "already" and "not yet" as aspects of God's Kingdom. This tension will always remain until Christ returns.

Peter's revelation and confession that Jesus Christ is Lord is the foundation and cornerstone of the church (see Matt. 16:18-19). No sooner had Simon Peter confessed this great revelation to His Master, he stumbles over truths relating to Jesus' death. Jesus rebukes him, saying, "Get behind Me, Satan! You are an offense to Me, for you are not mindful of the things of God, but the things of men" (Matt. 16:23).

The words *hindrance* or *stumbling block* refer to something that makes one stumble or is the reason for a fall (cf. Matt. 11:6). The response Jesus made to Peter conveys an important truth for addressing the false. Like Peter, anyone can communicate great truth, but within moments become a stumbling block, saying something false.

With these in mind, it is obvious that one is not necessarily heretical by conveying what is false, but church authority should correct the person disseminating false doctrine so others will not stumble. This requires confronting the error but also giving place for change and growth in the person. This should cause every Christian to cling to humility, and not become a stumbling block to others.

Judging Doctrines, Ministries, and Leadership

Judging doctrines and ministries is not easy but it's essential. Historically those who moved with convictions of the Spirit often went against certain doctrines and practices of the church. The early church also had disagreements, and the apostles Peter and Paul did not always see eye to eye. Therefore, guidelines for judging are not only helpful, but also necessary.

Now I urge you, brethren, note those who cause divisions and offenses, contrary to the doctrine which you learned, and avoid them.
—Rom. 16:17

Beware of false prophets, who come to you in sheep's clothing, but inwardly they are ravenous wolves.
—Matt. 7:15

A wolf is a natural enemy of sheep. A wolf in sheep's clothing is a metaphor that describes how the enemy comes to deceive and devour the sheep. Persons who claim to be true Christians can disguise themselves, but inside, their motives are to bring division and devour the sheep.

The church of Ephesus tested church leaders by looking beyond the surface to that of character. When men claimed to be apostles, the church of Ephesus collectively tested them and rejected their claim of apostleship. John the revelator wrote down the words of the Lord:

"I know your works, and labor, your patience, and that you cannot bear those who are evil. And you have tested those who say they are apostles and are not, and have found them liars."
—Rev. 2:2

Therefore, it is clear that Jesus holds the church accountable to judge those who claim to be apostles, prophets, and church leaders. John the revelator also recorded the Lord's rebuke of the church of Pergamus for allowing false leaders to infiltrate the church:

"But I have a few things against you, because you have there those who hold the doctrine of Balaam, who taught Balak to put a stumbling block before the children of Israel, to eat things sacrificed to idols, and to commit sexual immorality. 'Thus you also have those who hold the doctrine of the Nicolaitans, which thing I hate. Repent..."

—Rev. 2:14-16a

Persecution—from the Church, to the Church

When proper judgment happens, pressure and persecution are inevitable. Just as in His earthly ministry Jesus not only communicated the gospel of the Kingdom, He confronted a false gospel, distinguishing the Kingdom of God from what other religious leaders taught. Jesus often said, "You have heard it said, but I say unto you..." The religious leaders responded by sending Jesus to the cross.

During the Reformation, the Roman church responded to Martin Luther with excommunication. Likewise, in the formative years of the colonies in North America, many were persecuted, labeled heretics, and killed because they attempted to expose wrongs of the church. Therefore, there should be no surprise that as the church moves forward, proper judgment should take place. In addition to these judgments, there will be persecution, not from the world, but from the church.

Only in the End Is Distinction Clear

"Let both grow together until the harvest, and at the time of harvest I will say to the reapers, 'first gather together the tares and bind them in bundles to burn them, but gather the wheat into my barn.'"

—Matt. 13:30

Only at the end will separation between the true and false be complete, and until then, there will remain mixtures in the house of God. Even though the church seeks to guard and cleanse itself from contaminated mixtures, she cannot rid herself completely of them. As stated earlier, no person or group has a monopoly on truth, nor can anyone claim to be totally free from contamination of error.

Therefore, distinguishing the wheat from the tares can be difficult. God's reapers, the angels, however, have no difficulty separating them. The church should not overemphasize ridding the true from the false, but instead should seek to make a distinction by word and practice. Jesus tells the church to be patient and let them grow together, and in the end, He will separate.

Conclusion

Our witness to the world requires moving beyond the religious fights of liberals and conservatives, and subtle denominational disrespect that belittles important truths in others to esteem the importance of our own. The church must move beyond these to higher ground.

Every believer plays a part in moving the church forward. Not only should the church warn all believers against false Christianity, the church must equip them to represent true Christianity. They need messages to help them represent Christ.

Deception appears genuine, but requires a mixture of truth with error. "Naming the captivity" with which the church must contend requires more than identifying doctrinal error—it also requires identifying the spirit of error. When one can quickly identify errors in others but fails to see the errors in oneself, the snare of hypocrisy results.

This means that in the best of us there is error, and in the worst of us, there is some truth. And it is only in the end that it all becomes clear. In the meantime, we look through a glass darkly, seeking to represent the glory of Christ through human vessels of clay. This part of the Reformation is yet unfinished, and must move forward.

Questions for Further Research and Discussion

1. How does a Christian or a group of believers freely practice their convictions when they may differ from acceptable Christian doctrine, tradition, and practice?

2. What parameters distinguish the true from the false?

3. Who qualifies as the authority to distinguish the true from the false?

4. How might the church effectively practice excommunication to distinguish those that teach false doctrine in the spirit of error?

CHAPTER SEVEN

DISCIPLESHIP AND BODY MINISTRY

... breaking bread from house to house...

—Acts 2:46

Old Church and Body Ministry

THE SEPARATION OF clergy and laity, the priest and people, has created a passive people who are ill equipped for ministry. George Barna's list in the chapter on Worship describes the condition of body ministry.

Regarding Faith-Based Conversations...

- The typical believer will die without leading a single person to a personal relationship with Jesus Christ.
- At any given time, a majority of believers do not have a specific person in mind for whom they are praying for that person's salvation.
- Most Christians believe that since they do not have the gift of evangelism, outreach is not their responsibility.

Regarding Intentional Spiritual Growth...

- Only 9 percent of all born-again adults have a biblical worldview. Others have a patchwork theological perspective and rarely rely upon those views for daily decisions.
- The typical believer spends less time reading the Bible in a year than engaging in other leisure activities as watching television,

listening to music, reading other books and publications, and other things.

- When asked what constitutes success, few believers define success in spiritual terms.
- When given the opportunity to express how they wish to be known by others, one out of ten use descriptions that reflect their relationship with God. [118]

As believers actively participate as God's witness in the world then they will address the items in Barna's list. The church is the witnessing community as the people of God, and should move beyond gatherings on Sunday morning to become active witnesses in the world. Believers should become intentional about developing their relationship with God and communicating their faith experiences with others.

Warfare or Welfare Mentality

Oftentimes in church services people are entertained and not equipped. Persons often view ministry as spectators on the sideline instead of active players on the field. Too many attend church to watch the preacher preach, hear the choir sing, and never become actively involved in ministry themselves. This idea of ministry has produced a welfare mentality where believers do not take responsibility for ministry.

The other extreme of passive laity is the idea that involvement in ministry is the same as busyness in church activity. Some church leaders deliberately get people busy so as to keep them in church. The church keeps them busy, but does little to connect busyness with Christian growth and discipleship.

The body should be equipped and encouraged to participate in ministry. In this discourse, the author will continue to use the term *laity*, not for promoting the same strict separation from the *clergy*, but instead to communicate the idea that laypersons are the priesthood of believers who still require training from church leaders.

Return Ministry to the People of God

Donald G. Miller of Union Theological Seminary describes how there is a reverse of trend since the Reformation for encouraging laity to take responsibility for their own spiritual growth with personal devotion and study. He writes about this condition in the Foreword of Suzanne de Dietrich's book *The Witnessing Community*:

> Protestantism lives on the conviction that the Bible is the people's book. The Reformation put the Scriptures into the hands of laymen, and a smoldering faith burst into flame. A strange quirk of history, however, conspired to take the Bible away from laymen by the very movement that began in an effort to give it to them. The rise of critical study, with its demand for specialization in so many fields, tended to restrict the study of the Bible to the clergy and professional students of religion. Thus, once more the layman's knowledge of the Bible became limited to that which he received secondhand from others. [119]

Whether through the effects of critical study or something else, there is still a pervasive attitude that laypersons are inadequate for understanding the Scriptures. The problem is not the absence of the written Word or having the Scriptures translated in the vernacular of the common people. Bibles are available in many homes throughout America. Instead, the problem is in taking the written Word as the Living Word and allowing it to speak to individuals in their present day situations.

Until laypersons are equipped to engraft the Word into their lives, they will continue to be on the sidelines of Christian involvement, feeling ill equipped for giving witness to the world. The church becomes a better witness as all believers take seriously the written Word so it may become the Living Word in their hearts and lives.

Early Church and Body Ministry

When Jews or Gentiles decided to become Christians in the first century, they became dependent upon the Christian community for supplying all their needs in ways that the modern Christian, particularly in America, can scarcely imagine. The church had to assume almost total responsibility for the whole person in every aspect. The new believer truly became engrafted into the family of God. [120]

Even though individuals made personal commitments to Christ, they depended upon the entire Christian community for survival. As evidenced in the book of Acts, this ministry required more than the apostle and prophets. It required every member to be actively participating in body ministry.

Definition of *Body Ministry*

In the first-century church, the word minister did not refer to a title that represented a position for church leaders, but instead it meant a service rendered by the believer. Every believer ministered and served according to the gifts and graces each possessed.

Body ministry conveys the idea that just as every member of the natural body has purpose and is essential for contributing to the whole, so it is with the body of Christ. The apostle Paul describes the body of Christ as such:

> The manifestation of the Spirit is given to each one for the profit of all....
> For as the body is one and has many members, but all the members of
> that one body, being many, are one body, so also is Christ....But now
> God has set the members, each one of them, in the body just as he
> pleased....Now you are the body of Christ, and members individually.
> —1 Cor. 12:7, 12, 18, 27

Since God has set every member in the body, then each member should be properly set in connection with other members of the body. Unless each member is properly set, the whole body suffers because of it.

Freedom of Body Ministry

The first Christian community that formed beyond Jerusalem was in Antioch. The apostles did not begin this community. Instead, the witness of common believers sharing the message of salvation started it.

> Now those who were scattered after the persecution that arose over
> Stephen traveled as far as Phoenicia, Cyprus, and Antioch, preaching
> the word to no one but the Jews only. But some of them were men from
> Cyprus and Cyrene, who, when they had come to Antioch, spoke to
> the Hellenists, preaching the Lord Jesus. And the hand of the Lord was
> with them, and a great number believed and turned to the Lord.
> —Acts 11:19-21

The Christian community in Antioch subsequently became the capital and mission center to the Gentile world. When Christians were being scattered because of persecution; Stephen and others traveled to Antioch and shared the gospel. Believers were first called "Christians" in Antioch. This group developed into a Christian community.

Prevailing everywhere in Christian communities was new life full of promise. Through the work of the Holy Spirit, God used each believer to form the witnessing community. Though trained by the apostles, this community was not restrained or controlled by apostolic ministry. It became a "body ministry," each member functioning with each other for giving witness to the world.

Priesthood of Believers

> But you are a chosen generation, a royal priesthood, a holy nation, His own special people, that you may proclaim the praises of Him who called you out of darkness into His marvelous light, who once were not a people but are now the people of God…
>
> —1 Pet. 2:9,10a

Prior to the OT Levitical priesthood, the cultural trend for ministry was for the firstborn male child to be set aside for the Lord's service. However, through Moses, instead of firstborn males, the Levitical priesthood served in the temple. The priesthood becomes the mediator for Israel's relationship with God. Hence, through the priesthood, Israel is able to serve God and receives His blessing (see Zech. 3:1-5). Therefore, the essential function of the OT Levitical priesthood was to assure, maintain, and constantly reaffirm Israel as the elect people of God (see Exod. 28:38; Lev. 10:17; Num. 18:1).

The idea of the NT priesthood of all believers is erected in the early church from the OT, but distinct from it because Jesus Christ becomes the High Priest. Also in the NT, *priest* does not refer to some special group leading God's people. Instead, it involves the whole body of Christ, who are the special people of God, set apart for His purposes. Let's observe how these ideas of body ministry and the priesthood of believers changed through the course of history.

Historic Church and Body Ministry

Since most of the surviving documents of the church deal with the works and thoughts of church leaders, there is a tendency to forget that these writings present only a partial picture. There is another side of Christendom not well represented. Those who were not well educated, but were nevertheless believers, gave witness to the Christian faith. Therefore, when one attempts to reconstruct a picture of the early historic church, one faces an almost total lack of sources, and must be content with piecing together bits of information.

Most believers from the early historical church were from the lower social and economic strata. Therefore, writings relating to body ministry are very limited. It is safe to say that from the written historical sources, a picture of body ministry did not emerge until the Reformation period. Ideas of body ministry and the priesthood of believers had been lost. Instead, the clergy as the professional trained ministers served, while laypersons passively watched them.

For the most part, training for laity in the Roman church was limited to learning to serve in the church and assisting the priest in his sacramental duties. No training was toward preparing believers to be effective witnesses in the world. This, however, describes lay involvement in the institutional church, but aspects of lay ministry were also happening elsewhere.

Early Saints Movement

There had been much activity conveying the effects of body ministry in the early centuries of Christendom. By the year 100 AD, the church had been alive for seventy years, and three generations of Christian families existed. At the close of the first century, Christians had spread the gospel to millions.

In his book *The Day of the Saints*, Dr. Bill Hamon states that the church traveled in every land and in almost every city from the Tigris to the Euphrates Rivers, and from the Black Sea to North Africa. Over the next two centuries tens of millions more people became a part of the church. Many were martyred for their faith.

One of the reasons the church overcame the intense persecution of the early years is because of the faithful convictions of the saints, who functioned as servants and even slaves in Rome. Their witness of living from the teachings and ministry of Jesus had caused so many people to receive Christ that Christians were in the majority in Caesar's own household. God's people had invaded every aspect of society.

Bill Hamon notes:

The well-known letter of Pliny to the Emperor Trafan, written about AD 112, states that in the provinces of Asia Minor bordering the Black Sea the temples of the heathen gods were almost forsaken, and the Christians were everywhere a multitude. The standards of moral character were high and the supernatural power of God was being manifested by many Saints. [121]

Passive Obedience of the Laity

The Roman church clergy and laity separation developed a passive and obedient laity. This powerful structure of the Roman church produced believers who did not see themselves as "ministers" and did not exercise any effort for serving except through mediation of the church ordained priest.

The priest and clergy were so elevated in the church that they did not expect lay believers to read the Bible for themselves. Passive obedience to church leaders and participation in the sacraments became the concept for lay involvement. If one desired to serve in ministry, the only recourse was to train for the priesthood.

Not everyone accepted this idea, but the Roman church so dominated the idea of ministry that those who opposed it, like the Reformers of the sixteenth century, suffered excommunication.

Prior to the Reformation movement, beginning in 1517, the Roman Catholic Church and Eastern Orthodox Church did not allow its members to possess a Bible. One suffered severe punishment for having possession of the Scriptures. If one had a copy of the Scriptures, he probably could not understand it, since the Bible had not yet been translated into the language of the common people. The priests were the only ones qualified to read and interpret the Bible. Church members were completely dependent upon the priest. The average believer did not expect direct access to God.[122]

This established form of ministry made a great impact in shaping ideas for ministry. The clergy were distinct as the professionally trained, and expected to provide the immature laity with everything concerning ministry. This created a passive people where *priesthood* referred to the professional, instead of the ministry of every believer.

Reformation and Priesthood of Believers

In response to Roman church practice of priest and laity, the Reformers taught that every Christian believer was a priest in the service of God and could approach God's throne without the assistance of any human priest. Instead, through Jesus Christ, our High Priest, every believer has access. In other words, the Reformers taught that in having a personal relationship with God, every believer had the same rights, privileges, and responsibilities as the ordained, established priests. The Roman church branded the Reformers as heretics and eventually excommunicated them because of their position concerning the priesthood of believers.

The Reformers distinguished their idea of priesthood of believers from the Renaissance idea that "every Christian is a priest unto himself." Instead, for Reformers, every Christian is a priest to others in Christ, and they are priests to Him.

At the core of the Reformation movement was an attempt to change the institutional structure of church leadership. The idea of ministry under Roman Catholicism emphasized that receiving grace and receiving the sacraments were one and the same. No one could receive grace apart from the sacraments. This interpretation, therefore, made the hierarchy of priests dispensers of grace.

The Reformation, by contrast, linked the reception of grace with the gospel message and the response of faith for believing in Jesus Christ. Therefore, the church institution and its sacraments do not make one right with God, but right relationship with God happens through Jesus Christ. Neither pastors, bishops, archbishops, cardinals, nor the pope can represent an individual before God. Jesus Christ alone has that function.

With the rediscovery of the priesthood of believers, every Christian receives grace from God and becomes a minister of the gospel. The priesthood is not some superior calling to the ministry, but instead it belongs to the people of God. Therefore, believers should live with one another in social fellowship and demonstrate with others the works and practices of the Christian faith.

Moving toward a model for the priesthood of believers has not been easy. Luther seemed to affirm the priesthood of all believers sometimes and take it away at other times. Greg Ogden quotes Luther: "We are all priests insofar as we are Christians, but those whom we call priests are ministers selected from our midst to act in our name, and their priesthood is our ministry." [123]

Institutional Entrapments of the Reformers

The Reformed concept of the church had great potential for change, but only produced a measure of freedom before being engrossed with other challenges for reforming the church. As a result, instead of equipping all believers to be active participants in ministry, passive laity continued. Reformers focused their attention not on developing laity but on gaining political support to withstand Roman church power and authority. For support, the Reformers sought to intertwine their new ideas of church authority with that of state authority.

For example, the principles of the Reformed church in Zurich, Switzerland, under Ulrich Zwingli's influence, led to the merger of church and city government. This structure used civil authority to enforce moral responsibility. Thus, since the Reformers had difficulty practicing what they believed in theory, they put restraints on the freedom they had once encouraged and institutional entrapments continued to hold believers in captivity.

From the time of Constantine at the turn of the fourth century to the ratification of the U.S. Constitution, it was an unchallenged assumption that the church needed the coercive power of the state to enforce its teachings and establish social order. Therefore, Zwingli instituted in Zurich a church order supported by the coercive power of civil government. The government required by law every citizen in Zurich to conform to this new evangelical message preached by Zwingli.

Thus, when John Calvin refined church order in Geneva, he identified four officers that should lead the church. He identified pastors, teachers, deacons, and elders. Elders, as he saw them, consisted of twelve city officials. They shared the responsibility of enforcing church discipline with city councils. Local officials had the authority to both appoint and discipline its ministers.

The Reformed or state churches developed according to geographic boundaries and the civil authorities governing those boundaries. In order to be a part of the city or state, one was required to submit to the established religion of that locale. Church and state authorities were hopelessly intertwined.

The American Religious Experiment

America is unique and distinct in its idea of separation of church and state, where the state shall not make any laws mandating its citizens to commit to any religion. Otherwise, freedom of religion is a concept that has not seen much development throughout history.

The Reformers did not liberate the idea of priesthood of all believers into a new form of church order and structure. Even though they challenged the old Roman church structure, there has been very little, if any, movement toward any new order of recognition of a true priesthood of believers.

Even in America, institutional entrapments of the established church have not loosened very much. The church must develop a model for equipping and releasing the people of God to do the work of ministry, and thereby enabling the church to grow.

It is still true that the model of ministry in the minds of most churches is one in which the minister is the dominant pastoral superstar who is equipped to do ministry, while the laity are spectators and recipients of ministry, who are free to go about their own way because the pastor is taking care of the work of ministry.

The Wesleyan Model, An Attempt to Move Forward

As stated previously, John Wesley made no claims to setting up local meetings or "societies" with a NT ecclesiastical structure. Instead, he designed his model of leadership to be practical for fulfilling the Great Commission of reaching the lost.

As distinct from and in opposition to the established Church of England, Wesley organized societies who met in private homes with leaders, mostly women and untrained clergy, to lead in weekly home devotions with up to eleven others. This allowed many who were not active participants in the church to serve in a leadership role. The movement grew rapidly and led to the use of lay preachers who were not ordained. Their function was parallel to the sacramental function of ordained priestly ministry in the Church of England.

From these small groups emerged the idea of accountable discipleship. This happens when believers give one another permission to speak the truth in love, helping each person follow through with their commitments to God. To make accountability effective, regular contact with one another is necessary. Accountable discipleship is as follows:

> This is mutual accountability where each member holds each other accountable. In Wesley's class meetings, these weekly gatherings were first and foremost designed to equip Christians to be authentically Christian in a world which was largely hostile to their message. The early Methodists believed that they had received a direct commission to go into the world, and to join the risen Christ in the task of proclaiming God's salvation in the power of the Holy Spirit. The class meeting was where they came to share the bumps and bruises of this encounter, to comfort and strengthen one another, and to provide a mutual accountability for the task in hand. [124]

If there is one word the world hates, it is the word *accountability.* The prevailing attitude of many in the church is similar to the humanistic idea that everyone is a priest unto himself. They shun the idea of being accountable to anyone. However, the essence of Christian discipleship requires personal responsibility and communal accountability.

Specific Considerations for Continued Reformation

In his book *The Unfinished Reformation,* Morrison addresses the authoritarian institution of the Roman church and offers the following ideas concerning reformation:

1. The depersonalization of the individual believer should be replaced with personal fulfillment and actual participation in the ministry of the church and in the world.
2. The passive obedience of the Catholic laity should be replaced with active responsibility of the laity in ministry involvement in the church. In the Protestant church, laity continues to have little responsibility in ecclesiastical functions.
3. Unity with diversity must replace unity by uniformity. Protestantism anchors its faith in the revelation of God in Jesus Christ. It therefore welcomes diversities and differences that do not dislodge or dissolve that supreme event. It finds the inspiration of spiritual life in the unending unique experiences and reconciling these differences in the expectation that new experiences and insights will emerge from person to person, group to group, and age to age.
4. Unity based upon a superficial morality should be replaced with morality of personal depth and dignity. Protestantism has rejected the whole system of ethics embodied in the institution of penance. It sees ethical superficiality of the system and the hypocrisy and moral complacency that it breeds. [125]

In contrast to the Roman church's elaborate system of the sacraments for managing the moral life, Protestantism points the believer directly to God who deals with personal faith, sincere repentance, and holy living. The way to God is through Jesus Christ and not impeded by any priestly mediator.

New Church and Body Ministry

Before Christ returns in His glory, He will be glorified in and through His church. Just as the first-century apostles remained in Jerusalem while the saints went everywhere proclaiming the gospel and manifesting the power and glory of the resurrected Lord, the saints will once again go everywhere reaping the great harvest, and apostolic ministries will follow up by equipping new converts to fulfill the ministry of the priesthood of believers (see Acts 4:14; 10:44).

New Wine in the Same Old Wineskins

What began over five hundred years ago during the Reformation is yet unfinished. Clericalism still identifies Protestant church ministry with the separation of pulpit and pew. Many Protestant denominations have been as divided in clergy/laity ministry as the Roman church. The minister, as bishop and pastor, has remained elevated, while spiritual gifts and body ministry have largely remained dormant.

The Roman church hierarchical system and the Protestant denominational system have the same effect: They each hold the true church captive. As the Reformers sought to liberate the true church from the façade of the hierarchical institution, so must the Protestant church today remove the façade of preacher/pew ministry for liberating the people of God.

There has been an awareness of this captivity, and some have explored ideas for moving forward. The question that Ogden asked still screams for an answer today: "Why didn't the new wine of the gospel produce the new wineskins of body ministry? What kept the Reformers from returning the ministry to the people of God?"[126] Why didn't the idea of priesthood of believers develop into a model to be implemented?

The Unfinished Reformation

The Reformers challenged the institutional church with its top-down governmental structure and ordained priestly ministry. However, there is still much development needed for returning ministry to the people of God.

Jesus did not build the church with the religious leaders of His day, but instead went to young men who simply believed His message. Those who gathered on the day of Pentecost were not the leaders of the community but were ordinary believers who simply heard and obeyed the message. The Holy Spirit then showered them with an outpouring of power that no human institution can claim.

So it will be in moving from Reformation to restoration, where common believers hear the gospel, believe it, act upon it, and take responsibility for fulfilling their ministries in the world. Unless the old wineskin becomes flexible enough to contain the new wine, it will burst through it. What may appear as uncontrolled, out of order chaos for some may in fact be a new release of freedom and power for finishing the unfinished Reformation.

The unfinished Reformation must not only deal with separating from a legalistic religious structure, but also for allowing the people of God to move toward freedom in ministry. This move will require proper spiritual oversight for giving foundation and guidance, but maintain the focus for returning ministry to the people.

The attempt to graft a concept of priesthood ministry of the people of God onto established forms of ordained ministry has not really worked. A more appropriate approach is to reaffirm that all ministry happens by the Holy Spirit's endowment of gifts upon members of the body. Ministry titles are not necessary, but may be used to describe particular functions, not positions of power.

This concept requires viewing the church as an organism, observing the life evident in the smallest parts, with each giving life to the whole. As an organism, each member works together with all other members.

Governmental authority working with the Holy Spirit guides and properly connects each member with others in the body. This is a mysterious and sacramental relationship that values the oversight of eldership and the priestly ministry of believers. Then the glory of Christ will be seen in and through His body.

Since the Reformation, there has been little change in developing new wineskins that can contain this new wine. Liberation does not come easily. Those believers who recognize the entrapments of the institutional church organization, and desire to see change must be prepared to engage in spiritual warfare to set God's people free.

Church Government and Freedom of Body Ministry

> But the saints of the Most High shall receive the kingdom, and possess the kingdom forever, even forever and ever....Until the Ancient of Days

came, and a judgment was made in favor of the saints of the Most High,
and the time came for the saints to possess the kingdom.
—Dan. 7:18, 22

As previously stated, the Bible makes no distinction between clergy
and laity. The separation of the classes developed relatively early in
the history of the church. The Bible does distinguish mature elders for
giving oversight and equipping the priesthood of believers (see Eph.
4). The priesthood of believers requires mutual interaction of freedom
and accountability for guidance, consolation, instruction, confession,
forgiveness, and even discipline.

Body ministry must not develop without some form of ecclesiastical
leadership structure, but there will come a shift in the way church leaders view church members. There is a grass roots movement of hungry
believers who desire to be more effective in their witness to impact the
world. Instead of being preoccupied with leadership titles, positions,
and power, there will be a focus on returning ministry to the people of
God. In doing so, freedom of the believer will balance with structure
and accountability.

Structure and divine order are as eternal as Christ and His church.
The church will have structure and order that does not hinder freedom
of personal conviction and responsibility. The new church that seeks
ministry of all believers will not be without leadership authority, but will
have leaders that promote body ministry.

Suzanne de Dietrich describes this community as our true witness
to the world.

> Our firm belief is that it is part of the calling of the church to show the
> world what true community means: a fellowship of free persons bound
> to one another by a common calling and a common service. Only in
> Christ can we solve the tension between freedom and authority, between
> the right of the individual person to attain fullness of life and the
> claim of the community as a whole on each of its members. For in and
> through him we learn what it means to be perfectly free, yet obedient
> unto death; to come as a servant, yet through this very self-abasement
> to attain fullness of life. [127]

In the broad sense, the Holy Spirit instills life in the church, producing
new freedom enjoyed by every believer. Were not our churches and
denominations founded on this pursuit of freedom? Does not each
denomination desire to experience a self-governing body, living according

to its own practices, beliefs, and convictions? This pursuit of freedom will continue, but it must have balance.

The true church therefore becomes free because it recognizes that man-made structures in denominations have their place, but are not final authority. Instead, the rule of Christ as Head in God's Kingdom is final authority.

This freedom happens through the governance of the Holy Spirit, which has both structure and freedom. As the natural body has a structural system that enables the body to move freely, so must the body of Christ have structure to experience its true freedom. The focus, therefore, is not on organization, but on organism.

Organization and Organism

The Reformers had the theory of priesthood of believers but not the application. Its language spoke of the organism within, but developing ways to display this organism through church organization was another matter. The Reformers sought different models, but none emphasized the workings of body ministry as a living organism.

A new approach from the hierarchical model would require viewing body ministry not from the top down, neither from the body up, but from the authority of Christ, the Head, through the Holy Spirit, working through all believers for promoting His will in the earth. In this case, every member functions in their areas of gifts and passions for benefitting the whole. The structure of the organization should not stifle the life of the organism, but instead enable its life to find expression through its structure.

The life and community of this organism is where believers are truly free and subject to God alone. With this freedom comes submission and accountability to others. These work in unison because each believer becomes aware of each other for representing Christ through His body. The thing that is most characteristic of this new freedom is that it involves bringing persons out of isolation and connecting them in true community (see Acts 2:37-47; 4:23-37).

Balance Freedom with Accountability

The essential question that separates Protestant and Roman Catholic thought is this: Does ecclesiastical order represent some attribute of Christ Himself that the church should maintain, or is it a means to an end for something greater? If church order and structure represent some attribute of Christ the church must maintain, then it must also include a freedom of the Spirit so as to liberate every member to properly function in body ministry.

The church is very resilient and it has withstood the test of time. Two key elements have kept its resilience over the years: the convictions of freedom of the Spirit and the respect for church authority. The church must keep these two in delicate balance. Freedom without discipline leads to chaos. But on the other hand, structure without freedom leads to bondage and stagnation. Structure nails down, while freedom lifts up. Freedom of the Spirit and ecclesiastical accountability are an ongoing tension, but the two must remain in delicate balance for the church to be who she was intended to be.

Church organization is not an end, but it is important for moving toward something greater—to complete the unfinished work of the church. Since the body of Christ is a living organism, not an organization, setting a framework could become a hindrance if it does not emphasize body ministry. Organization exists to promote the life of the organism.

Just as a baby is born with all essential elements needed for growth, so does the church also have all her essential elements. Concerning both, the mature appearance of the child as well as that of the church, one can only speculate. Thus, we search for a structure whereby the child, the church, may continue to receive proper nurture for growth to maturity.

Equip the Saints: From Information and Activation

> Churches that don't equip and release the saints will become less relevant, and eventually empty, religious institutions.[128]

The historic church has focused on believing right doctrine. Informational truths are important. However, these are not the end of the message. Just as important is connecting right belief with right action, and with information should come demonstration and activation.

The church is called to equip, prepare, mend, put in proper alignment, supply what is lacking, establish, and supply developmental training for each person to grow to maturity for reproducing leaders to help others become disciples. An equipping church is therefore a training center.

The end should be application of those truths into everyday life. Just because one is unable to articulate their faith in acceptable educational rhetoric does not mean they are unable to qualify for eldership and church leadership. They can develop those skills. Many can demonstrate with simple faith the power of the gospel, and therefore have value for leading others. The church should identify and utilize these for leading others.

A Revolution in the Making

If the unfinished Reformation does not expeditiously move toward restoration, there will be a revolution. This entails a violent outburst of new wine released from old wineskins. Just like Jesus confronted the religious order of His day, this revolution will be a confrontation against a religious system that can no longer keep God's people captive.

This revolution will not begin with an organization, but instead it's a movement of people hungering for more. Like the Renaissance and Reformation, people moved to radically denounce structures of the old so something new would come forth. Likewise, if old structures refuse to change, the church today will again experience this type of revolution.

In *Revolution*, George Barna describes this transition of church structure. He portrays this movement as many mini-movements already evident in transforming the church. As mentioned previously, this transformation evolves from believers seeking new ways for practicing their Christian faith.

These mini-movements are evident in homeschooling, simple house fellowships, various market place ministries, spiritual discipline networks, creative arts, and other movements seeking to express their faith without ecclesiastical politics and oversight.

A disturbing observation Barna makes is that the mini-movement phenomenon includes millions of Christians who are passionate and demonstrate their faith, and the local church is not—and need not be—the epicenter of their spiritual adventure. [129]

A serious concern from Barna's assessment of how the church is changing is that he sees little or no importance for proper church leadership needed for equipping the saints. Neither does his model emphasize key concepts of Christian development such as commitment, submission, doctrine, correction, rebuke, and instruction in righteousness (see 2 Tim. 3:16).

NT affirms leadership in the church. The early apostles appointed elders in every church (Acts 14:23; Titus 1:5). Paul writes these words to the Thessalonians:

We urge you, brethren, to recognize those who labor among you, and are over you in the Lord and admonish you, and to esteem them very highly in love for their work's sake...

—1 Thess. 5:12-13

Barna's idea of revolution does not include these aspects of leadership in the transformation of the church.

Conclusion

Just as a child must not be left alone to grow but grows under the guidance and nurture of parents, so must every believer have leaders to guide and nurture that growth. According to the Scriptures, the church becomes the "perfect bride" with church leadership equipping believers to do the work of the ministry (see Eph. 4:12).

Unless the church develops new wineskins to contain the new wine, denominational and church structures will witness violent transformations. Church leaders and seminary institutions should be warned—change is happening, whether we like it or not. Tensions that come with change may cause uncertainty and resistance, but if it is the work of the Spirit moving the church forward, then the church must not resist the wind of the Spirit. The winds of change are blowing, and the church must not miss this grand opportunity for change. Be warned. Be encouraged. Get ready. The new church is coming forth.

Questions for Further Research and Discussion

1. Describe the importance of distinguishing between making good church members in comparison to and contrast with making disciples of Christ.

2. Describe how the ministry of the priesthood of believers should look.

3. How should the body work together for doing the work of the ministry?

4. Describe central components of ministry for balancing freedom with accountability.

5. What are the key elements needed for equipping believers for body ministry?

CHAPTER EIGHT

REVIVAL OR REVOLUTION?

... And the Lord added to the church daily...

—Acts 2:46

Old Church Need for Revival

EVANGELISM AND SALVATION have always been central components of the church. However, their expressions have varied. As stated throughout this discourse, and especially in the first chapter, there is need for the church to reevaluate important truths and hold firm to those truths in times of transition.

This section is challenging, because it's one thing to analyze and affirm certain truths, but another to demonstrate the power of those truths. Revival, reform, and revolutions all have mysterious aspects that demonstrate the power of the gospel for church growth and Kingdom advancement. Even though church growth is happening in many parts of the world, it's a mystery that some churches and denominations see only marginal or no growth.

In addition to examining the extent of growth, we should address how church growth affects society. One view of evangelism focuses on just winning souls for heaven. This view provides little or no information for equipping believers for ministry in the world. It sees the world as a "ship sinking fast," and holds that the church should save as many as possible before the ship goes down.

The other end of the spectrum sees salvation happening through a social gospel. This view places little or no emphasis on personal salvation but instead seeks to bring healing and well-being to society. People who subscribe to this definition of salvation have often pressured governmental entities to provide support for those in need.

Between these ideas of salvation is a variety of ways the church seeks to take the gospel throughout the world to make disciples and to prepare for the return of Christ. Therefore, many Christians view history as salvation history, where God works through the redemptive work of Christ for progressively bringing salvation to the world.

Through the death, burial, and resurrection of Jesus Christ, the Kingdom has drawn near, and the church has received a foretaste of it. Henceforth, the church now pursues with unshaken confidence and expectations the new heavens and a new earth which are to come (see 2 Pet. 3:13; Isa. 65:17). The church will at last see the Lord face-to-face, and more completely understand what has not been previously understood. "We shall be like Him, for we shall see Him as He is" (1 John 3:2).

Until this time comes, the church lives expectantly, learning to submit to the Lordship of Christ and fulfilling the mission He has given. The first generation of Christians believed the return of Christ was imminent. For a long time the apostle Paul himself shared such conviction, but then exhorted believers to be patient, urging them to keep working with their daily tasks. Evangelism and growth, in some mysterious ways, point toward the completion of all things at the end of the world. Until such time, the church must work toward that expected end.

As we consider, "What does God want?" the church must move forward with a profound awareness of what Christ has already accomplished and how the Kingdom of God will reveal Christ as Lord of lords and King of kings. This realization leads to the importance of evangelism, discipleship, revivals, awakenings, revolutions, the "restoration of all things," and the end of the world.

Revivals and Church Growth

Revival closely relates to church growth; yet understanding that relationship is unclear. Under some conditions revival may cause growth. Under others, growth happens without revival. Careful consideration of the subject is essential for understanding the function of each in God's purpose of redemption. [130]

The word *revival* has many connotations. To some, revival among the elite and intellectual is associated with a distasteful trait of emotional outburst and disorderly conduct of the lower classes. To others, revival refers to planned church services, where guest speakers come in to minister. Revival also refers to a purification and revitalization of the existing church. To another group with which the author identifies, revival refers to unplanned extended gatherings where large numbers are converted, and unusual behaviors of signs, wonders, miracles, and healings are reported. This type of revival eventually leads to awakenings and reform where new ideological constructs form and societies transform.

Wagner/McGavran cites J. Edwin Orr, who has done extensive research on revivals. Orr relates revivals with evangelical awakenings. He says:

> An Evangelical Awakening is a movement of the Holy Spirit in the church of Christ bringing about a revival of New Testament Christianity. Such an awakening may change in a significant way an individual only; or it may affect a larger group of people; or it may move a congregation, or the churches of a city or district, or the whole body of believers throughout a country or continent; or indeed the larger body of believers throughout the world. Such an awakening may run its course briefly, or it may last a whole lifetime (Orr 1965:265). [131]

Revolution, Movements of Chaos

When revival transforms individuals, but does not transform religious and social structures, seeds of revolution exist. Revolution is not necessarily the opposite of revival, but a more violent means for moving toward a common end—to arouse in the mindsets of society the need for supernatural intervention for solutions to existing problems. If revival does not change old structures, possibilities for revolution increase.

Present Day Evangelism

There is a nonchalant attitude among believers when it comes to evangelism, outreach, and discipleship. Many continue to expect ordained ministers and evangelists to win others to Christ. The idea of the priesthood of believers is still embryonic when it comes to believers demonstrating their faith in word and action. They are uncomfortable with leading others to Christ.

As previously noted, according to Barna's research, eight out of ten who attend church do not feel they regularly experience the presence of God. Half of all believers say they have not experienced a genuine connection or presence of God within the past year.

If people do not sense the presence of God in churches, then why do they come? They may come out of obligation rather than out of expecting to experience God's presence. If this is the case, then it is understandable why believers are not excited about evangelism. If they are not experiencing the presence of God, then they will not be excited about inviting others to experience the presence of God.

Hindrances to Revival and Growth

What might be some reasons some churches or regions experience revivals and growth while others do not? McGavran identifies some possible hindrances:

1. Too many glorify slow growth. McGavran notes that some theologies and evangelistic methods look askance at rapid growth. Too many glorify slow growth by making statements like these:

    - We do sound work and are not interested in shortcuts.
    - It takes decades to grow an oak. A pumpkin grows in a single summer.
    - God takes his own time to make a sound church.
    - The field, maintained at great cost and agony over many years, often proves to be the seedbed from which a rich harvest comes.
    - Soundness of growth, not rapidity, is the criterion. [132]

      These statements assume that good growth requires slow growth and that the quantity of labor guarantees the quality of the product. Nothing in the Bible or growth of New Testament churches supports this assumption.

2. Remnant theology proves attractive. A glorification of littleness prevails, in which to be small is to be holy. Slow growth is adjudged good growth.

    Christians believe that they should be passionately concerned that the church be a church made up of committed Christians, but if we make smallness our goal, are we true to Him who preached the gospel to multitudes? If we make a select company the goal, are we in danger being pharisaical and holier-than-thou?

Does being a Christian happen by ethical achievement or is it a redemptive relationship to Jesus Christ? [133]

3. Discipling and Perfecting—McGavran acknowledges that standard dictionaries do not list *disciple* as a verb, but he started using it in 1955 in his book *The Bridges of God*. It meant helping people turn from non-Christian faith to Christ. His comments are instructive:

> Discipling was to be followed by perfecting, that is, by the whole complex process of growth in grace, ethical improvement, and the conversion of individuals in that first and succeeding generations.[134]

McGavran goes on to describe how the use of the term *disciple* has evolved to include several meanings. First, discipleship means turning a non-Christian for the first time to Christ. Secondly, discipleship refers to incorporating them into the church. Third, discipleship means teaching Christians as many truths of the Bible as possible.

4. Quality and Quantity—There is no question that all Christians can experience a deeper life of faith and grace. However, the least mature church is better than its non-Christian origin. McGavran states:

> Some earnest Christians reject multiplication of churches as today's chief task because they pin their hopes on quality rather than quantity. What use, they ask, to make more Christians unless they are *better* Christians? Throughout much of the world they affirm that education of believers is more important than evangelism. In America, they assert that church unity is more important than church extension.
>
> We must inspect closely this attractive plea for quality. As soon as we separate quality from the deepest passion of our Lord, to seek and save the lost, it ceases to be Christian quality....To fight for brotherhood is good; but to proclaim that brotherhood is more important than salvation is misguided. [135]

The church must remember that we are not called to serve an imaginary, ideal, perfect church. We are required to participate in the church-as-it-is, with all of its grandeur and all of its misery—holy and sanctified, yet comprised of sinners in need of grace. The church's imperfections belong to us, just as our imperfections belong to it. And it is with these imperfections that the church lives, struggles, suffers, and hopes to be delivered.

In Need of Revival

Conditions in America today are ripe for revival. Ideologies and constructs of yesterday are not solving the problems of today. Historically, when America faced such conditions, revivals gave birth to awakenings and reforms that transformed society. People gained new awareness of the presence of God being in their midst. Times are ripe for this to happen again.

North America, some believe, is a difficult field for revival. Indifference to Christ and His church seems to be the attitude of many. Pluralistic ideas and Western religions have their appeal as viable alternatives for spiritual development. Generational and contextual trends are blamed for empty pews. Some believe the church will continue declining and Christianity will continue weakening in its influence in the world. To some, these are signs that the world is coming to the end. To others, however, these are times ripe for revival.

Early Church Revival and Church Growth

The Birth of the Church

The early church was a revival movement, birthed in the midst of great tensions around it. Those who followed Jesus to His death and waited for the promise of Pentecost faced great tension and conflict. Leaving Judaism meant they also left the support of their families and communities. Evidence of this is seen in the generosity of each believer willing to share what he had with others in the community (see Acts 2:44-46).

Therefore, this new community waited in the Upper Room in faith. Their waiting for something new was not passive, but active and desperate.

A Restoration of All Things

The early church was conscious of living at the dawn of a new era. This created radical expectations that were not concerned with temporary reforms. At the core of this new era was something basic—the death and resurrection of the old world and the creation of the new in Christ (see 2 Cor. 5:17). There were significant ideas that promoted this new era.

The church was not concerned with a flight or Rapture into a hereafter, but with the coming of the reign of Christ, with an entirely new order of things that directs all governments, all institutions, and all men to the one Lord. The restoration of all things looks forward to the reign of Christ to rule the world. The church's birth of Christian community is the beginning of this restoration (see Acts 3:19-23).

Even though this restoration and the coming Kingdom is hidden in God's wisdom, Christians in the early church did not passively wait for it, but instead became active participants, having a foretaste of this new Kingdom, and by faith lived in its reality with hope of seeing the fullness of the Kingdom manifested in their lifetime.

The Gospel Preached throughout the World

Clearly seen from the gospels is concern and zeal for reaching the lost. All the early church's preaching, even when aimed at those within the church community, had the stamp of evangelism and missionary activity. The church carried the message of repentance throughout the world, and this message somehow connected to bringing fulfillment to the restoration of all things.

Although the gospels of Matthew and Mark are not missionary writings in the narrow sense, they address the Christian community with its missionary mandate. These missions went beyond Israel to the Gentile people throughout the world (see Matt. 28:19, 20; Mark 16:15, 16).

Before going into the world, Jesus instructed His disciples to wait in Jerusalem for power. On the Day of Pentecost Jews representing every nation were present, and within the first century Christians spread the gospel throughout the world.

And there were dwelling in Jerusalem Jews, devout men, from every nation under heaven.

—Acts 2:5

Because of the hope which is laid up for you in heaven, of which you heard before in the world of the truth of the gospel which has come to you, as it has also in all the world.

—Col. 1:5, 6a

For the grace of God that brings salvation has appeared to all men.

—Titus 2:11

Body Ministry with Apostolic Support

Early church growth came from a people's movement, but apostolic authority was necessary for correction and discipline. Notice how this happens from these passages:

…At that time a great persecution arose against the church which was at Jerusalem; and they were all scattered throughout the regions of Judea and Samaria, except the apostles.

—Acts 8:1

Therefore those who were scattered went everywhere preaching the word. Then Philip went down to the city of Samaria and preached Christ to them.…And there was great joy in that city.

—Acts 8:4, 5, 8

Now when the apostles who were at Jerusalem heard that Samaria had received the word of God, they sent Peter and John to them.

—Acts 8:14

And when Simon saw that through the laying on of the apostles' hands the Holy Spirit was given, he offered them money.

—Acts 8:18

But Peter said to him, "Your money perish with you, because you thought that the gift of God could be purchased with money!…You have neither part nor portion in this matter, for your heart is not right in the sight of God.…For I see that you are poisoned by bitterness and bound by iniquity."

—Acts 8:20, 21, 23

Having been scattered by persecutions, Philip went to Samaria, preaching the gospel and demonstrating its power. The city rejoiced from having witnessed the power of God with signs and miracles and turned to Christ. Simon, a sorcerer, amazed by the miracles, also received Christ, and followed Philip.

When the apostles from Jerusalem heard of "revival" in Samaria, they sent Peter and John. The apostles ministered by the laying on of hands, the gift of the Holy Spirit. When Simon saw this, he wanted to pay money for this power. The apostles recognized the wrong spirit and rebuked him.

This correction was essential for revival to continue moving in the right direction. Body ministry with apostolic authority and support is a good model for moving the church forward toward evangelism, discipleship, revival, and church growth.

On the other hand, body ministry without apostolic support is a picture of *revolution*—a movement that despises and shuns authority. This is the idea Barna describes in *The Revolution*. Revolution confronts old authoritative structures, and unless these structures address the concerns of the people, there is chaos. Let's observe these trends in church history.

Historic Church Revivals and Revolutions

Salvation and Evangelism

Historically, the gospel message has touched the hearts of people to be delivered from the "old" and transformed into the "new." Struggles for change have not only brought personal change to individuals but have also confronted established ideologies and authoritative structures with the message of change.

When the disciples went out, they preached Jesus, and those who believed became a part of the church. From history, we shall observe individual struggles that led to personal salvation and the social and cultural tensions from which revivals and awakenings emerged.

Evangelism emphasizes sharing the gospel to move unbelievers to commit to Christ and accept the Bible for its authority. *Evangelicalism* as used today describes those Christians who proclaim that each person should hear the gospel message of salvation through Jesus Christ. Even though evangelical churches have not always adopted the practices of ecstasy and emotionalism often associated in charismatic moves of the Holy Spirit, both have reached unbelievers with the gospel for personal salvation.

As previously noted in the chapter *Preeminence of the Holy Spirit*, when there is freedom to follow one's conscience to be "led by the Spirit," there is also room for error. Growth of the church will always have to deal with wheat and tares, sheep and goats, gold and stubble. Therefore, in evangelism and church growth, the true and false will manifest together, and in a mysterious way, this imperfect church moves toward becoming the perfect bride for the Bridegroom. Many times these ways for salvation, growth, and purification are evident through revivals.

We shall observe salvation and revivals in two ways. First, we shall note how individuals struggled with their quest for personal and corporate salvation. Then we shall observe revivals and awakenings throughout American history. The intention is to shine some light on addressing the issues facing the North American Protestant church today, and how God may be using these challenges to move the church and the world closer toward His unfolding plan.

Individual and Corporate Ideas of Salvation

Monasticism: Salvation Apart from This World

The Monastic view of salvation raises the concern that the church oftentimes becomes too much like the world, and many seek solitude apart from the church. They seek to fulfill something they are not receiving from the church. This raises the awareness of tension between one's spiritual hunger and the abundance of church traditions and organizational "stuff" that clashes with it. Many today leave the established church for the same reason monks in earlier years did.

Those who fled to monasteries believed that true happiness is not in having the material things of the world but in the service of God. They believed that one renders that service best when one breaks from the glories with the world. Dress, food, and other necessities become as simple as possible, and one devotes oneself entirely to prayer. Ambrose, Bishop of Milan, was an example of this tension.

In the early stages of the historic church, while some church leaders pushed politically for positions of power, Ambrose fled to the monastery to avoid being made bishop. Later, he was consecrated Bishop of Milan in 373. During this period many refugees ravaged by war with the Goths flocked to Milan. Ambrose responded by ordering that funds be raised for the refugees by melting golden vessels and other ornaments the church possessed.

Ambrose's writings reflect his attitude toward the world in these words:

> It is better to preserve for the Lord souls rather than gold. He who sent the apostles without gold also gathered the churches without gold. The church has gold, not to store it, but to give it up, to use it for those who are in need....It is better to keep the living vessels, than the golden one. [136]

Salvation: Augustine's Struggle of Inner Conflict

Augustine saw evil as being both around him and in him. He struggled with the source of such evil. This awareness of inner conflict moved Augustine to search for answers. He reasoned this way:

> When I thought of devoting myself entirely to you, my God...It was I that wished to do it, and I that wished not to do it. It was I. And since I neither completely wished, nor completely refused, I fought against myself and tore myself to pieces. [137]

One of his major works, *Confessions,* is a spiritual autobiography, a type of prayer addressed to God that tells how God led him in faith through a long and painful pilgrimage.

Augustine's ideas of salvation have had tremendous impact on church doctrines. The church should continue to communicate this inner struggle for finding salvation and peace within.

Salvation: the Roman Catholic Sacramental Approach

Sacramental liturgy as practiced by the Roman church dispenses grace through the priest to the recipient. While some shun the idea of looking to priest for salvation, others seem to benefit from it. As stated previously during the Renaissance and Reformation, individual freedom and inner conviction confronted this sacramental way of salvation. However, untold millions are committed to such practices today.

Those who shunned the Roman Catholic's idea of salvation through the sacramental system desired more personal and subjective aspects of salvation, like the humanists and later the Reformers taught.

Salvation: Erasmus and the Humanist Approach

Prior to the Protestant Reformation, a passing away of the old and the coming forth of something new had already begun. This included ways of searching for truth, especially ways of finding peace within. In search of new concepts concerning salvation, old ideas were threatened.

Erasmus of Rotterdam, called the "Prince of Humanists," was the forerunner. Taking an approach similar to the Monastic's concern for inner spiritual development and Augustine's struggle within, Erasmus was convinced that Christian conflict was an inner one. Erasmus believed that while outward means such as the sacraments were important and should not be discarded, their significance was in their inner meaning conveyed to the heart of the believer.

Erasmus claimed the following:

> What the church needs, in order to be reformed, is for Christians to practice this discipline, and to abandon the vices of pagans....Erasmus had in mind the evil example set by the popes of the Renaissance, who would rather be compared to Jupiter or with Julius Cesar than with Jesus or St. Peter.

> "What good is it to be outwardly sprinkled with holy water, if one is filthy within?" In short, what Erasmus sought was the reformation of customs, the practice of decency and moderation, an inner devotion shaped by learning and meditation, and a church that encouraged these things. [138]

Toward the end of the Middle Ages, the rise of humanism evolved into mystical piety, searching for truths to quiet the conflict within. The mystics believed that all one had to do was to love God, and that all other tensions and struggles would follow as a result of that love.

Salvation: Luther's Justification by Faith

The Reformers sought to communicate the mysterious workings of grace and its effect for salvation. The idea of justification by faith stirred radical ways of thinking about salvation. This concept focused on the believer's individual faith and personal relationship with God for finding peace within.

Luther had difficulty loving a God whom he perceived to be a disciplinary father. As demonstrated by his teachers who had beaten him to the point of drawing blood, Luther desired to find peace with a loving God, but discovered hatred toward a disciplinary God!

The practice of sacraments did not resolve this conflict. Luther saw no way out of the difficulty. On the one hand he wanted to love God, but on the other, he saw God as Judge. His spiritual advisors recommended that he read the great teachers of mysticism. Becoming familiar with these teachings, Luther sought the monastic lifestyle, seeking to ease the conflict within.

In his discovery from reading the Scriptures, one found peace in being "justified by faith." Luther discovered that through faith in the redemptive work of Christ, salvation is a free gift for all who believe.

From this discovery, Luther described his experience:

> I felt that I had been born anew and that the gates of heaven had been opened. The whole of Scripture gained a new meaning. And from that point on the phrase "the justice of God" no longer filled me with hatred, but rather became unspeakably sweet by virtue of a great love. [139]

Predestination: Why Be Concerned?

Predestination has been a point of discussion within the church. It carries the idea that God's sovereignty has already chosen those whom He has predestined to save. Varying degrees of the doctrine of predestination have shaped the church's understanding of salvation. Two streams of thought include Calvinism and Arminianism.

One of John Calvin's main points of theology is God's sovereignty. In pursuit of His ultimate purpose God allowed man to sin, although man did so according to his own will. Through His predestined plan, God in His grace purposed to redeem men from their sin and bring them to His glory.

Calvin described predestination this way:

> These people are those whom God has chosen in Jesus Christ from all eternity, not with any prevision of their faith or righteousness, but solely of His own free grace of love. No man would of himself turn in repentance and faith to God, because of the corruption of his sinful nature, unless God by the Holy Spirit should regenerate him...[140]

To Calvin, man's reconciliation is all of God and of God's sovereign grace. Thus, the elect can never be lost, but will persevere until the very end. For those who accept this position, the sovereignty of God also involves a basic ethical principle. It is God's sovereignty that causes man to be truly responsible for ethics and morality. God, the Sovereign Lord and Creator of all, initiates men to serve Him in all they do.

Jacobus Arminius, a Dutch theologian (1560-1609), opposed Calvin's teachings of predestination. This conflict divided the student body of the seminaries as well as ministers of the Reformed church.

After the death of Arminius, his followers outlined five major points of Arminianism. These include that (1) Salvation applies to all who believe on Christ and who persevere in obedience and faith; (2) Christ died for all men; (3) The Holy Spirit must help men to do things that are truly good; (4) God's saving grace is not irresistible; and (5) It is possible for Christians to fall from grace. [141]

The teachings of Arminianism greatly influenced the idea of salvation for others. John Wesley followed this belief, and it left its mark on the Methodist church. Even those with a Calvinist heritage continue to discuss the points that Arminius raised.

Salvation: Individual or Social?

Individual salvation is a fairly unique concept more readily accepted in America today than at any other time in history. The Renaissance and Reformation periods raised the idea of individual and subjective inward convictions as important elements of salvation. Some cultures around the world as well as throughout history know little or nothing of individualized decision-making processes, so common in the West. In those cultures, families or communities are involved in important decisions.

During the Constantine era, being Christian meant serving the religious/political and church/state agenda. With the Roman Catholic Church, salvation referred to the church and emperors aligning to promote and enforce the interests of church and state. During the Reformation, however, persons identified with ideas of salvation by geographic areas of residence. These also sought secular authority for enforcement of Christian ideas.

Thus personal salvation is a fairly unique phenomena more readily practiced in America than in any other place and time in history. Other nations and cultures respect individual salvation, but not with the degree of emphasis with which it is practiced in America. In many other countries, the emphasis is on community, not on the individual.

Convictions of personal faith coupled with a desire to bring the salvation message to others gave birth to awakenings and reforms. Those with such convictions eventually confronted authoritative structures and affected social change resulting in new ideological constructs. In an attempt to ascertain possible clues for future movements, let's now examine how revivals in North America have helped shape and impact society and its history.

Revivals and Awakenings in American History

Since the forming of America in Jamestown in 1607, revivals and awakenings have helped shape mindsets, societies, and the course of American history. There have been at least four or five of these awakenings that have dramatically affected the shaping of this nation. Tremendous growth in the church existed in periods of religious and social tensions, and this growth affected change in both.

At the heart of forming this nation was the idea of being a chosen people with a manifest destiny to lead and demonstrate to the world the concept of democratic-republic institutions, and how free and morally responsible individuals can operate under high moral and what many believe to be Christian laws. Revivals and awakenings have had their share in promoting freedom for not only the individual and nation, but also the world.

The essay *Revivals, Awakenings, and Reform* describes these American movements. It is obvious that these revivals and awakenings came in periods of great tension, conflict, and crisis.

From the forming of American colonies, awakenings have helped shape the American culture. The awakenings, without holding strictly to dates, include these: the Puritan Awakening 1610-1640, the First Great Awakening 1730-1760, the Second Great Awakening 1800-1830, the Third Great Awakening 1890-1920, and the Fourth Great Awakening 1960-1990(?).

William McLoughlin describes periods of awakenings as periods of cultural revitalization that begin with a clash of beliefs and values and may extend over a period of a generation or so. During this period a profound reorientation in beliefs and values takes place. He says;

Revivals alter the lives of individuals; awakenings alter the world view of a whole people or culture: [142]

Great awakenings (and the revivals that are part of them) are the results...of critical disjunctions in our self-understanding. They are not brief outbursts of mass emotionalism by one group or another but profound cultural transformation affecting all Americans and extending over a generation or more....Great awakenings are not periods of social neurosis (though they begin in times of cultural confusion). They are times of revitalization. [143]

In short, great awakenings are periods when social, economic, political, and cultural systems face challenges to revitalize in order to overcome jarring disjunctions between experiential norms where old beliefs and dying patterns clash with emerging new patterns of thought and behavior.

The Puritan Awakening (1610-1640)

America's inception as a nation came through an awakening. Its settlers arose from the tremendous energy unleashed in the Puritan movement. It took a profound commitment to doing God's will and faith in His oversight to move tens of thousands of men, women, and children to uproot themselves from their homes and embark on a journey in cramped ships through frigid weather and treacherous conditions toward the New World. The first settlers were driven by conscience, faith, and hope for better conditions.

Ideas of Puritanism clashed with old established ideologies of the Church of England. Beginning with its quarrel over the purification of the Church of England, the Puritan movement spread to include a host of other political and economic issues. By 1630, it brought to surface basic dysfunctions within society and critical things the church needed address.

Eventually, Puritan concepts spread among the common people. The commoners took literally the concept of direct communion with God and the power of grace to transform the hearts of individuals. This concept included the possibilities of social reformation and the creation of God's Kingdom on earth.

There was a strong element of individualism in the Puritan creed. This tension between individual freedom and social order Edmund S. Morgan calls "the Puritan dilemma."[144] The established Church of England considered them rebels, but in order to practice their ideas of a new society, the Puritans had to restrain the rebellion of those in their midst. The conflict between the demands of authority and the permissiveness of freedom continued as polar tensions of the American culture core.

The First Great Awakening, 1730-1760

The American Revolution came on the heels of the First Great Awakening. This movement helped join the thirteen colonies into a cohesive unit. The awakening gave the colonies a sense of unique nationality and inspired them with the belief that they were, "and ought to be," a free and independent people.

Prior to this awakening there had been a falling-off of conversions. Times were generally prosperous, and those who worked hard could make their way in the world. They saw material success and the rewards of prestige and power as signs that their ways of living were acceptable to God. While few experienced "saving grace," the majority felt they were no worse than any other. Ministers regretted the lack of conversions, but preached that ultimately God in His own way and time would save the souls of His elect.

In light of the times, by 1720 the older order was under severe stress. The old ideological framework of church/state authority was losing its cultural legitimacy, and there was a search for new loyalties. In doing so, revival broke out.

Americans were oriented toward Calvinistic ideas (probably three-fourths of the colonists). They fully believed that they deserved to be "cast into hell" for their disobedience to God's commands. Yet, beginning in 1734, God seemed to mercifully extend forgiveness and salvation to thousands. When Jonathan Edwards described the revival outbreak as "a surprising work of God," he spoke for most Americans.

Massive and continuous revival meetings were in motion from 1740 to 1745. Out of the awakening emerged new churches and new forms of Christian fellowship. Individual freedom and fraternal union of fellowship went hand in hand. This new sense of brotherhood and sisterhood expressed a new awareness of covenant and community. Out of the ecstasy of regenerated souls came the idea of common union of all in service to God.

The awakening began when itinerant though ordained preachers offered new styles of preaching and a new rhetoric that called people back to God. The enthusiasm aroused by these itinerant men also inspired imitators. Sometimes persons who were not ordained but felt an internal call preached the gospel in a new way.

The itinerant preaching of the Reverend George Whitefield was perhaps the major contributor to the general outbreak. He had established a reputation as a sensational preacher in England, and had the advantage of carrying with him the authority of church ordination. Whitefield de-emphasized the institutional side of religion and emphasized the personal responsibility for each person to be right with God. With this method, Whitefield witnessed many conversions.

Itinerants such as Whitefield, delivered the gospel in a new medium—the spoken word of the common man. Lay preachers who preached without formal education meant that ordinary people were speaking to each other with new authority. Their power did not come from academic degrees, ordinations by some clerical body, or from the established upper class, but simply from the Spirit of God. These preachers did not bother to seek admission to local pulpits, but delivered their messages in private homes, in the marketplace, in barns, schoolhouses, and open fields. A new kind of religious leadership emerged.

Another important aspect of this awakening is how Arian ideologies remained within the state churches as "liberal" or "rational" ideas found their place in prominent places of higher education. These denied the necessity of a conversion experience and believed that all could attain salvation by leading moral, honest, respectable lives of love for God and for one another.

Arian theologies represented by the Unitarians in Boston and Harvard as well as by the Church of England were committed to the concept of salvation by education, church ordinances, and moralistic self-discipline.

Jonathan Edwards, considered the leading theologian of the First Great Awakening, helped lead the way to a new consensus. He criticized the radical "new lights" as taught in many schools of theology.

The Second Great Awakening (1800-1830)

The leading prophet of the Second Great Awakening was Charles G. Finney. Though the dominant ideology was still fundamentally Calvinist, a message of salvation emerged with a new definition leaning toward perfectionist theology.

Finney's view of salvation held that the reborn must become unselfish or totally altruistic. "All sin," appeals to selfishness, and all holiness and virtue, one finds through benevolent living. Regeneration, therefore, is a change from selfishness to benevolence, from having supreme regard to one's own interest to an absorbing will and joy for bringing glory to God in the service of others. This meant that the reborn are committed to sacrificing their pleasures to advance God's Kingdom on earth and prepare the world for the imminent return of Christ.

One significant clash of the old and new during the Second Awakening is that through the American Constitution, the government "...shall make no law respecting an establishment of religion, or prohibiting the free exercise thereof." The church now faces the challenge of finding ways to motivate persons to commit to local fellowships without civil authority intervention. Revival meetings could not only be successful in forming new churches, but could also find ways to sustain the socializing power of camp meetings and disperse its harmonizing power throughout other communities.

The Third Great Awakening (1890-1920)

Important changes of this period were in technology and mass communications. These included cheap penny newspapers that gave detailed coverage of revival meetings.

D.L. Moody, probably the first Fundamentalist, maintained a pessimistic, premillennial tone that characterized the reaction to the societal and cultural crises of the period. In one sermon in 1877, he said; "I look upon this world as a wrecked vessel.... God has given me a lifeboat and said to me, 'Moody, save all you can.'" [145]

Billy Sunday was also an important figure of this era. He stood in the center of the cultural confusion with the fears that science and evolution threatened ideas of God's law and creation.

During the years from 1890 to 1920, evolution and the pragmatic philosophy of the "new social sciences"—particularly the behaviorist and Freudian psychological theories—seemed to undermine the core beliefs of Christianity as evangelicals understood it. Billy Sunday attacked the new scientific theories, and in so doing, he preached a message that represented the fears and confusion of millions of American Christians.

The Social Gospel Movement

During this period, ideas of salvation manifested in various streams, with the social gospel also making its impact. The social gospel got its name because it argued that men must come to God not as "atomistic individuals," but as united to the brotherhood of mankind, in which each is spiritually and ethically connected.

Theologically, the social gospel message came perilously close to Pelagianism—the belief that through one's own efforts and good works one can achieve his own salvation. Followers of the social gospel justified their faith not in terms of the miraculous birth and resurrection of Jesus but by the role of Jesus in human history as the perfect human ideal Christians should imitate.

McLoughlin quotes Walter Rauschenbusch, the foremost leader of the social gospel, who asserts that the source of evil has lain in the preoccupation of Protestant evangelicalism with soul-winning and revivalism. He summed up the problem facing America as "the wrongful abandonment or the perversion of the great aim of Christ—the kingdom of God." He comments:

> Because the Kingdom has been dropped as the primary and complete aim of Christianity and personal salvation has been substituted for it, therefore men seek to save their own souls and...the individualistic conception of personal salvation has pushed out of sight the collective idea of a Kingdom of God on earth, and Christian men...are comparatively indifferent to the spread of the spirit of Christ in the political, industrial, social, scientific and artistic life of humanity. [146]

The Fourth Great Awakening (1960-1990?)

The religious reaction against pragmatic liberalism emerged from a group of Protestants who urged returning to more orthodox views of Christian faith. Originating with Karl Barth and led by Reinhold and Richard Niebuhr and Paul Tillich, the neo-orthodox ideology was a type of Christian realism that distinguished itself from the unrealistic, fuzzy-minded idealism of liberal Protestantism.

In addition to these, the '60s also produced a new shift in our belief-value system. It transformed our worldview in ways that may be the most drastic in our history as a nation. Individual freedom driven by the idea of having "love and peace" with all mankind resisted all authoritative structures that frustrated this freedom. The Vietnam War brought serious doubt about our mission in world affairs and manifest destiny as a nation. Also, there arose a striking new interest in ideologies of the East as those of the West lost influence for giving meaning to life.

Once again, the American culture is suffering from a crisis of legitimacy. Old norms do not satisfy daily experience and people are seeking new paradigms. Beliefs and values are under pressure to adjust to changing ideas. Americans are uncertain of their future and frightened over their inability to cope with a world so complex and unpredictable.

Trying to understand and pursue the future of the church is merely "looking through a glass darkly." These descriptions of evangelism, revivals, awakenings, and reform are only a small portion describing historical trends of how the church seeks to fulfill the Great Commission within the complexity of cultural changes, tensions, and crises. Seeds of what is to come have been planted and will continue to grow into manifestation, if not by revival and reformation, then by radical revolution.

New Church—Revival or Revolution?

A Denominational Dilemma

Many churches and mainline denominations are searching for answers. Membership has fallen and ways to communicate central truths to the current generation come with certain challenges. Many denominations are undergoing critical examination as they seek to continue the mission and mandate.

The United Methodist Church is one example of this ongoing critique. In two decades from 1965 to 1985, the United Methodist Church lost two million members. Its emphasis was social action, brotherhood, peace, and other such causes. Evangelism and church planting were low. It became obvious that unless the decline reversed, the denomination would continue its decline in membership and influence.

The Methodist church appointed George G. Hunter III, professor for evangelism at Perkins School of Theology in Texas, and gave him a quarter million dollars a year budget with a mandate to reverse the downward trend. He studied every aspect of the decline, and under his guidance the Methodist church started to see a quantitative difference in their denomination.[147]

What's Next?

Revival does not happen in a vacuum. Neither do movements and change happen smoothly. Instead they happen when a generation faces challenges, and old structures and ideologies no longer satisfactorily address those challenges. In times of prosperity, when things go well, people become comfortable and do not seek God. However, when life begins to tear at the seams, people search for new ways of believing and living.

Many today are very uncomfortable. Ideologies and constructs of yesterday do not solve the problems of today. Every system—governmental, economic, educational, religious, social, and psychological—faces challenges, accompanied by structures that worked yesterday but do not work today. Convictions of the heart eventually lead to revival, reformation, or radical revolution.

Pressures facing the church in America today threaten not only the church but America's very existence. The church's eschatological convictions of coming into something new will confront old ideologies and systemic structures. This change does not only come from the learned and trained, but also from the unlearned and untrained whose convictions are bold enough to challenge old religious, political, and social constructs.

Reinhold Niebuhr describes Christianity's ability to persist through chaos and effect change:

> The Christian religion, in its profoundest terms, is a faith in the meaningfulness of existence which is able to defy the chaos of any moment, because the basis of its trust is not in any of the constructs of human genius or any of the achievement of human diligence .... Hence periods of prosperity inevitably lead to the corruption of the Christian faith, while periods of adversity prompt men to probe more deeply into the nature and meaning of human life....Thus periods of adversity are the seasons of a genuine renewal of the Christian religion. [148]

In the first years of the twenty-first century, tensions between the old and new have increased. The conditions facing America today follow evolutionary trends described by William McLoughlin for coping and surviving during periods of chaos and crises. In his book *Revivals, Awakenings, and Reform*, McLoughlin utilizes concepts of cultural change described by the anthropologist Anthony Wallace in his essay "Revitalization Moments" (*American Anthropology*, 1956).[149]

1. *The first stage is individual stress.*

This stage happens when parents can no longer guide their lives and children, when churches and schools no longer provide consistent ethical guidelines for social behavior, and when the courts no longer support sanctions deemed just and acceptable with traditional values.

One by one, people lose their bearings, become psychically or physically ill, showing signs of neurosis, psychosis, or madness. Some may break out in acts of violence against family, friends, and authorities. The old has begun coming apart at the seams. [150]

2. *The second is a period of cultural distortion.*

Gradually people conclude that the problems they face are not personal but are resulting from institutional and systemic malfunctions. Schools do not maintain discipline over their pupils; the police and courts cannot maintain order; and churches have difficulty offering comfort and strategies for the challenges people face.

In every culture there are stress-reduction mechanisms built into it. Some turn to church with appeals to God, some seek medical assistance from doctors and guidance from counselors, and there are other legitimate outlets as in recreation and sports. However, in periods of cultural distortion ordinary techniques to reduce stress no longer work and the populace is at odds with itself. The people cannot cope with stress and severe personality disorders are widespread.

When a culture functions harmoniously it is able to cope with natural disasters such as floods, earthquakes, epidemics, and economic dislocations. However, in periods of cultural distortion, people cannot agree and work together for coping with the dangers. They quarrel, divide, and blame those in authority. They refuse to unite. [151]

3. *The third is that new mazeways formulate into new senses of reality.*

Mazeways, according to Wallace, are the imbued cultural patterns of thought and behavior that guide individuals in their daily lives.

> At the basis of any culture is a generally understood and accepted world view by which each adult orients himself or herself to the family, the neighbors, the employers, the rulers, the social order in general. Through the child-rearing process the individual learns what his role is in his own town and what his place is in the universal scheme of things. He learns that he should act in conformity with man-made laws because they are the ways prescribed by the power that controls the universe. [152]

A revival or awakening begins when accumulated pressures of the old clash with a need for something new. Such acute personal and social stresses develop that society seeks new ways for believing and acting, thus forming new mazeways. Those under stress must seek those individuals who can help them formulate a new consensus and create new mazeways.

These new mazeways must be in harmony not only with daily experience but also with the way in which that experience reflects the realities of the mysterious power at work throughout the universe. [153]

4.   The fourth and final stage happens when new mazeways emerge with newly formed ideologies and restructured old institutional systems. The most rigid who hold firm to affinities of the old will find this transition difficult. They continue as much as possible to follow the old ways, but eventually they represent the minority. They gradually drift into the new consensus when they find it more satisfactory or conclude that they can no longer sustain the old order.[154]

The church faces challenges today, but these are not limited to the church. The church is merely in the midst of tensions of old structures tearing apart at the seams because they no longer satisfy. Historically, revivals, awakenings, reforms, and revolutions, with new mazeways, emerged to provide a new consensus of reality. The church will discover new mazeways as it pursues the unfinished work of God's unfolding purpose.

Unfinished Business

America is on the verge of revival or revolution. In all awakenings, the concept of God's immanent presence as opposed to God's transcendence becomes distinguished. Therefore, the task of the church today is to seek God's manifested presence in the midst of our challenges.

In America, it seems that the first stage of individual stress as McLoughlin describes has already moved into the second stage of cultural distortion. The next stage is one of new leadership who can produce new ideas and constructs for creating new mazeways.

Without being overly concerned with the time this move began, several important trends are unfinished. During the 1960s, religious leaders like Billy Graham, Oral Roberts, and Kathryn Kuhlman resurrected the traditional mass revivalism in the cities. Dr. Martin Luther King, Jr. emerged to raise awareness toward the nation's social ills of injustices and economic inequalities. Tensions from the 1960s also demonstrated resistance to civil and religious authority and old structures.

The church did not move very far from old patterns. Those who did not desire the old ideas and practices of the church found new interest in Zen Buddhism, magic, astrology, Satanism, and the occult. While some turned to reaffirm their Judeo-Christian heritage, many young people turned elsewhere in search for inner peace and love for everyone. In rebellion to authoritative structures, including the church, many experimented with drugs and music in search for inner peace, and some preferred the practices of eastern religions.

Elements of revival and renewal continued in the '70s and '80s. The Center of World Mission announced that more people came to Christ worldwide since 1980 until today, as compared to those who came prior to this period, since the beginning of the church. [155] However, from these revivals and church growth, new mazeways have not translated into new constructs for affecting systemic structures and institutions. There have been new ideas and methodologies for affecting systemic structures, but these have not yet affected society in America like previous revivals and awakenings.

Revivalism and the Unfinished Reformation

In putting this unfinished business within a larger framework, the church continues to face unfinished business from the Reformation period. There is yet disjunction between freedom of the individual and ecclesiastical accountability. There is still too large a separation between priest and laity. There is still much work needed for equipping each member of the body to be passionate about fulfilling the great commission. There is still much work needed in demonstrating unity in the church. Lastly, but not least there is also much development needed for giving the Holy Spirit rightful place of preeminence and authority in the church.

Since the Reformation, the process of God's unfolding work becomes evident through history. The Reformation was not only a movement for that period but also a movement for generations that followed. It began but did not complete important things for moving the church forward.

The church now faces need for another movement, distinct but connected to previous ones. It should complete the unfinished business. An ongoing dilemma of growth in the Christian community is in dealing with the struggle between freedom of expression and restraining of its excesses. This tension is an uncomfortable reality that ultimately leads to bringing change in individuals, communities, societies, nations, and therefore history.

The church must not only accept such tensions. The church has the ability to use these tensions for birthing something new. The eschatological tension of the "already" and "not yet" is an essential work of the Spirit in the life of the church.

Historians generally assume that the failure to reform is either because of too many vested interests or the lack of coordination in the reforming coalition. This will eventually lead to a greater upheaval or even revolution. [156]

The many challenges facing America today must not distract the church from completing the unfinished work. Since institutional systems must adjust, it's important for the church to lead the way in influencing new models to affect other authoritative systems.

An Unfolding Revelation and Manifestation of God's Kingdom

> The God of heaven will set up a kingdom which shall never be destroyed…it shall break in pieces and consume all these kingdoms, and it shall stand forever.
>
> —Dan. 2:44b

Daniel prophesied of God's Kingdom, and the early church accepted it as an unfolding of God's plan and purpose. The coming of Christ and the birth of the church ushered in God's Kingdom, and this Kingdom will grow to subdue all things. The church must remember that God is revealing and unfolding His plan throughout human history. The ultimate goal of history is the *new creation*, a creation filled with all the fullness of God where Christ rules in God's Kingdom.

Through Jesus Christ, the Kingdom has come near, and the church has received a foretaste of it. In the meantime it waits with unshaken confidence and actively pursues and celebrates God working through His church for bringing forth "new heavens and a new earth in which righteousness dwells" (see 2 Peter 3:13; Isa. 65:17).

Conclusion

One of the deepest mysteries of the Christian faith is that salvation procured by Jesus Christ on the cross is not only salvation for the individual but it has cosmic ramifications. Through redemption, the whole creation which was once condemned for death is now redeemed to newness of life.

There have been and will continue to be diverse ideas of how the mature church should be. The church continues to look through a dark glass, and it remains unclear how the glorious mature church, the bride of Christ, will look on that day. In the meantime, the church should actively pursue models, concepts, and mazeways for promoting that end.

Until Christ returns in His full glory, the church will go through periods of change. These changes lead toward growth and maturity, becoming the perfect bride of Christ.

Times of tension toward chaos and confusion are also opportunities for revival, reformation, and restoration. Old structures cannot contain new moves birthed by the Spirit. Therefore, the challenge of the church today is to seize upon this season of change, and complete the unfinished work of the Reformation. The church must faithfully pursue making new wineskins, new mazeways and structures, to contain the new wine.

Questions for Further Research and Discussion

1. How might periods of tension in American history be opportunities for revival and church growth?

2. Since this nation protects the idea of freedom of religion, how should the church respond to the increase of interest in Eastern religions in America?

3. Is Christianity losing its influence in this nation? If so, how does this affect the church's fulfillment of the Great Commission?

4. Describe how salvation and revival should also effect change in society and the world.

CHAPTER NINE

CLOSING THOUGHTS

THIS DISCOURSE HAS probably raised and stirred more questions than it has answered. I hope it has provided enough information for further research and discussion. No one person or group has all the answers, but the Holy Spirit working though the body of Christ, His church, has the answer. As we address the challenges facing the church and world, let us affirm some essential truths.

Learning from History

At the end of the first century, Ignatius, the Bishop of Antioch, organized the church in such a way that separated the idea of ministry from the people of God and directed it to the professional clergy. For centuries, the people of God depended upon others for their spiritual development, and in doing so became a passive people.

Trends for returning ministry to the people of God and enabling all believers to pursue their spiritual development are essential. The Renaissance, Enlightenment, and Reformation highlighted the importance of the individual and personal relationship and responsibility. Other trends include the translation of the Bible into the languages of the common people.

However, since the Reformation period there has been little movement. Instead, the church has evolved into many fellowships and denominations, and returning ministry to the people of God has developed very little.

This is the unfinished business the church must move toward. Returning ministry to the people of God is not without church government, authority, and leadership, but there is equal focus on every member being respected and utilized for body ministry.

Faith expressions will continue in both subjective personal convictions and outward manifestations in loyal commitment with other members in service to the Kingdom of God. These things will happen by the Spirit, where the church realizes the resurrected power of the Lord.

Get Ready—Change Is Happening

Missions to the world, growth of the church, and the coming of God's Kingdom do not happen passively, but by conflict, sacrifice, suffering, and persecution. The Kingdom of God suffers violence, and the violent take it by force. According to the early and historic church, God sometimes allows persecutions and tensions to stir the church to do what she is afraid to do on her own.

A mysterious undercurrent is flowing right before our eyes. In the midst of the church there is a move within various denominations and assemblies that have a greater appreciation of the church that transcends denominational and local church affinities. Many believers desire another level for respecting various expressions of faith where they can enjoy the richness of Christ realized in His body.

By the Holy Spirit

There is a move of the Spirit bringing growth throughout the world. This growth is not always within the organized denominations, but the impact of Christianity is growing. The fastest movement in the church is what has traditionally been associated with Pentecostalism.

This project has enlightened me to the evidence of moves of the Spirit in many denominations, but many have not always celebrated moves of the Spirit. Baptist, Methodist, Presbyterian, Episcopal, and even the Roman Catholic churches have moves of the Spirit in their histories, but for some reasons have shunned or minimized the importance of such expressions.

It's time for the church to come to terms with mysterious ways of the Spirit that stretch the church beyond its doctrines and traditions. As noted throughout this discourse, there should be foundational truths and organizational structures, but these must not restrict moves of the Spirit. Instead, they must guide and channel those moves in proper direction for the church to grow. This involves more than preparation to "go up"—it involves preparation to "grow up."

In addition to this, it was worth noting that after using Rudolf Schnackenburg's book *The Church in the New Testament* significantly throughout this discourse, I discovered that he was a Catholic priest. His writings were very helpful for gaining a better understanding of the early church. Also the objective for his book is the same as my own. He says, "This study is intended to promote mutual discussion. It is not meant as the last word on any of the questions touched upon, some of which are still vigorously disputed."[157]

The Glory of His Body

> Behold what manner of love the Father has bestowed on us, that we should be called children of God! Therefore the world does not know us, because it did not know Him. Beloved, now we are children of God; and it has not yet been revealed what we shall be, but we know that when He is revealed, we shall be like Him, for we shall see Him as He is.
>
> —1 John 3:1,2

> And the glory which You have given Me I have given to them, that they may be one just as We are one.
>
> —John 17:22

In His earthly ministry, persons related to Jesus on different levels depending on how they viewed Him. To Peter, James, and John on the Mount of Transfiguration, there was a revelation and relationship. To the twelve, there was a different level of revelation and relationship. To the seventy, there was another level of revelation and relationship. To the masses, there was another. And to Peter, there was yet another.

Likewise, this same Jesus reveals Himself to individuals, local assemblies, nations, and generations to the degree they are ready to receive Him. The challenge facing the church in America today is to prepare to see Jesus in ways He wants to uniquely reveal Himself to this nation, where His church plays a vital role. Our church eschatology has not placed enough attention on the glory of God yet to be revealed in His church.

This closing thought is worth remembering. At the wedding feast of the Lamb, attention is not on the Bridegroom but on the glory of the bride. This does not take away the glory of the Bridegroom, but the glory of the bride reflects the glory of the Bridegroom in such a way that great heavenly host has attention on her, while her attention is toward Him, and His toward her.

If the church is going to be ready, she must pay more attention to the glory of Christ being manifested in His body, the church. Before there is a Second Coming of Christ, there is a coming forth of the body of Christ.

Thanks for giving me an opportunity to share things I believe are important for the church today. The work of the church is yet unfinished and there is a burning within many believers who desire to see the church move forward. My prayer is that the church of today will not do what Ms. Berenstain Bear did. In going into the hat store, she showed every intention of desiring to wear a new hat. However, having become too familiar with her old hat, nothing new could satisfy. She left the store wearing the same old hat.

The church today has a grand opportunity for moving forward and taking a step toward fulfilling God's plan. This requires realizing that the old cannot contain the fullness of the new. The church is now in the store of opportunity, and my prayer is that she will leave wearing a "Brand New Hat."

ENDNOTES

1. Suzanne de Dietrich, *God's Unfolding Purpose, A Guide to the Study of the Bible* (Philadelphia: The Westminster Press, 1957), 17, 18.
2. Justo Gonzalez, *The Story of Christianity,* Vol.2 (New York: Harper and Row Publishers, 1984), 53. cites Conrad Grebel.
3. Mark Lawson, *It's the End of the Church as We Know It* (Pennsylvania: Destiny Image, 2007), 54.
4. Ibid., 59.
5. de Dietrich, 179-80.
6. See Milton, Leslie, *The New Century Bible Commentary, Ephesians* (Grand Rapids, MI: Eerdmans Publishing; London, Marshall, Morgan, & Scott, Reprinted 1989), 92.
7. See Merrill F. Unger & William White, *W. E. Vine, An Expository Dictionary of Biblical Words* (Nashville, TN: Thomas Nelson Publishers, 1985), 277.
8. Justo L. Gonzalez, *The Story of Christianity,* Vol. 1, *The Early Church to the Dawn of the Reformation* (New York: Harper and Row Publishers, 1984), 63.
9. Ibid, 63.
10. Ibid., 72.
11. Ibid., 63.
12. See Bill Hamon, *The Eternal Church, A Prophetic Look at the Church—Her History, Restoration, and Destiny* (Shippensburg, PA: Destiny Image, 1981), 122.
13. Charles Clayton Morrison, *The Unfinished Reformation* (New York: Harper & Brothers, 1953), 116.

14. Noah Webster, *American Dictionary of the English Language* (Foundation for American Christian Education, San Francisco, CA, 1828, fifteenth reprinting, 2002),

15. See J. D. Douglas, *The New International Dictionary of the Christian Church* (Grand Rapids, MI: Zondervan Publishing House, 1974, 1978), 808, 809.

16. See Hamon, *The Eternal Church*, 78.

17. de Dietrich, 21.

18. Ibid., 66-67.

19. Ibid., 229.

20. Lawson, *It's the End of the Church as We Know It*, 96.

21. See Merrill F. Unger & William White, *W. E. Vine*, 433.

22. Ibid., 443.

23. Lawson, *It's the End of the Church as we Know It*, 61.

24. Rudolf Schnackenburg, *The Church in the New Testament* (New York: The Seabury Press, First published in West Germany, 1965), 126-128.

25. Lawson, *It's the End of the Church as We Know It*, 116.

26. See Edward B. Cole, *The Baptist Heritage* (Elgin, IL:. David C. Cook Publishing, 1976), 113.

27. See Schnackenburg, *The Church in the New Testament*, 34, 35.

28. See Ibid., 27.

29. See Rick Joyner, *Shadows of Things to Come, A Prophetic Look at God's Unfolding Plan* (Nashville, TN: Thomas Nelson Publishers, 2001), 69, 70.

30. http://en.wikipedia.org/wiki/Ignatius of Antioch.

31. Greg Ogden, *The New Reformation, Returning Ministry to the People of God* (Grand Rapids, MI: Zondervan Publishing House, 1990), 66.

32. See Archibald Thomas Robertson, *Word Pictures in the New Testament*, Vol. VI, *General Epistles and The Revelation of John* (Nashville, TN: Broadman Press: 1933, renewal 1960), 98.

33. Ogden, *The New Reformation*, 48, 49.

34. Morrison, *The Unfinished Reformation*, 122.

35. Ibid.,105.

36. Ibid., 108.

37. Ibid., 110.

38. Ibid., 113-114.

39. See Cole, *The Baptist Heritage*, 111.

40. See Morrison, *The Unfinished Reformation*, 150, 151.

41. See Douglas, *The New International Dictionary of the Christian Church*, 227.

42. Ronald Patterson, Editor, *The Book of Discipline of the United Methodist Church* (United Methodist Publishing House, Nashville, Tennessee, 1988), 429-430.

43. Ibid., 32.

44. See Unger & White, *W. E. Vine*, 98, 129.

45. See Derek Prince, *Rediscovering God's Church* (UK: Derek Prince Ministries, 2006), 181-184.

46. Ibid., 187-88.

47. See George Barna, *Revolution, Worn-Out on Church? Finding Vibrant Faith Beyond the Walls of the Sanctuary* (Carol Stream, IL: Tyndale House Publishers, 2005), 22-24.

48. Ibid., 31-35.

49. See Schnackenburg, *The Church in the New Testament*, 21.

50. Ibid., 40.

51. See Gonzalez, *The Story of Christianity*, Vol. 1, 96.

52. Ibid., 100.

53. Webster, *American Dictionary of the English Language*, Fifteenth Printing, 2002.

54. http://en.wikipedia.org/wiki/Ignatius of Antioch/Letter to the Smyrnaeans 6:2–7:1.

55. http://en.wikipedia.org/wiki/Ordination of Women, Roman Catholic Church.

56. http://en.wikipedia.org/wiki/Thomas Aquinas.

57. Ogden, *The New Reformation*, 51.

58. David Yonggi Cho, *The Holy Spirit, My Senior Partner, Understanding the Holy Spirit & His Gifts* (Orlando, FL: Creation House, 1989), 18.

59. Ibid., 19.

60. A. W. Tozer, *Whatever Happened to Worship, A Call to True Worship* (Camp Hill, PA: Christian Publishings, 1985), 12.

61. Ibid., 26.

62. Ibid., 42.

63. Ibid., 31.

64. Ibid., 55, 56.

65. See Cho, *The Holy Spirit, My Senior Partner*, 19-20.

66. Ibid., 20.

67. Schnackenburg, *The Church in the New Testament*, 16.

68. See de Dietrich, *God's Unfolding Purpose*, 219.

69. See Justo L. Gonzalez, *The Story of Christianity*, Vol. II, *The Reformation to the Present Day* ((New York: Harper and Row Publishers, 1985), 196.
70. Gonzalez, *The Story of Christianity*, Vol. I, 136, 137.
71. Gonzalez, *The Story of Christianity*, Vol. II, 196.
72. Ibid., 201-202.
73. Ibid., 206-207.
74. Ibid., 210.
75. Ibid. , 212. Gonzalez cites Wesley's Journal, May 24, 1738.
76. Vinson Synan, *The Holiness-Pentecostal Movement in the United States* (Grand Rapids, MI: Eerdmans Publishing, 1971), 23-24.
77. Ibid., 26.
78. Ibid., 36.
79. Ibid., 50-51.
80. Ibid., 115-116.
81. Stanley Burgess and Gary McGee, *Dictionary of Pentecostal and Charismatic Movements* (Grand Rapids, MI: Zondervan Publishing House, 1988), 111.
82. Ibid., 261.
83. Ibid., 562.
84. Ibid., 48-49.
85. Ibid., 305.
86. See Martin E. Marty, *A Nation of Behaviors* (Chicago and London: University of Chicago Press, 1976), 1.
87. See Gonzalez, *The Story of Christianity*, Vol. II, 242.
88. H. Richard Niebuhr, Daniel D. Williams, and Sydney E. Ahlstrom, *The Ministry of Historical Perspectives* (San Francisco: Harper and Row Publishers, 1956, 1983), 12.
89. See http://en.wikipedia.org/wiki/Ignatius of Antioch.
90. Gonzalez, *The Story of Christianity*, Vol. I, 131-132.
91. Morrison, *The Unfinished Reformation*, 19, 20.
92. de Dietrich, *God's Unfolding Purpose*, 254.
93. Morrison, *The Unfinished Reformation*, 9.
94. Ibid., 71, 72.
95. Ibid., 73.
96. Edward B. Cole, *The Baptist Heritage*, 112.
97. Morrison, *The Unfinished Reformation*, 85.
98. Ibid., 87, 88.
99. Ibid., 19.
100. Ibid., 82.

101. Ibid., 129.
102. Avery Dulles, *Models of the Church* (New York: Doubleday Publishing, 1974), 124,125.
103. *Protection from Deception* (New Kensington, PA: Whitaker House, 2008), 169, 170.
104. Lawson, *It's the End of the Church as We Know It*, 188. Lawson cites Vance Havner, *Playing Marbles with Diamonds and Other Messages for America* (Grand Rapids, MI: Baker Publishing Group, 1985).
105. Michel Horton, *Christless Christianity, The Alternative Gospel of the American Church* (Grand Rapids, MI: Baker Publishing Group, 2008), 18.
106. Ibid., 50.
107. Ibid., 51.
108. Ibid., 29
109. Douglas, *The New International Dictionary of the Christian Church*, 464.
110. Ibid., 67.
111. Gonzalez, *The Story of Christianity,* Vol. I, 76.
112. Ibid., 53.
113. Ibid., 208.
114. See Ibid., 215.
115. Ibid., 214.
116. See Dulles, *Models of the Church*, 124, 125.
117. See Horton, *Christless Christianity*, 44.
118. See Barna, *Revolution*, 32.
119. de Dietrich, *The Witnessing Community* (Philadelphia: The Westminster Press, 1958), 9.
120. Niebuhr, Williams, Ahlstrom, *The Ministry of Historical Perspectives*, 12.
121. Bill Hamon, *The Day of Saints, Equipping Believers for Their Revolutionary Role in Ministry* (Shippensburg, PA: Destiny Image, 2002), 99.
122. Ibid., 20.
123. Ogden, *The New Reformation*, 52.
124. David Lowes Watson, *Accountable Discipleship, Handbook for Covenant Discipleship Groups in the Congregation* (Nashville, TN: Discipleship Resources, 1984, Revised 1986), 18.
125. Morrison, *The Unfinished Reformation*, 107-117.
126. Ogden, *The New Reformation*, 51.
127. de Dietrich, *The Witnessing Community*, 13, 14.

128. Lawson, *It's the End of the Church as We Know It,* 22.

129. See Barna, *Revolution,* 58.

130. See C. Peter Wagner and Donald A. McGavran, *Understanding Church Growth* (Grand Rapids, MI: William Eerdmans Publishing, 1970, 1980, 1990), 133.

131. Ibid., 134.

132. Ibid., 120.

133. Ibid., 21, 22.

134. Ibid., 123.

135. Ibid., 33-34.

136. Gonzalez, *The Story of Christianity,* Vol. I, 191. Gonzalez cites *Duties of the Clergy* 2.137.

137. Ibid., 207.

138. Justo L. Gonzalez, *The Story of Christianity,* Vol. II, 11.

139. Ibid., 20.

140. Douglas, *The New International Dictionary of the Christian Church,* 180-181.

141. Ibid., see 70.

142. William G. McLoughlin, *Revivals, Awakenings, and Reform* (Chicago, London: University of Chicago Press, 1978), xiii.

143. Ibid., 2.

144. Ibid., 35

145. Ibid., 144.

146. Ibid., 172.

147. See Wagner and McGavran, *Understanding Church Growth,* 277.

148. *Beyond Tragedy, Essays on the Christian Interpretation of History* (New York: Charles Scribner's Sons, 1937), 113-115.

149. *Revivals, Awakenings, and Reform,* 9,10.

150. Ibid., 12.

151. Ibid., 13.

152. Ibid,. 14.

153. Ibid., 15.

154. Ibid., 16.

155. Lawson, *It's the End of the Church as we Know It,* 115.

156. See http://en.wikipedia.org/wiki/ Christian Reform Movement of Europe.

157. Schnackenburg, *The Church in the New Testament,* 8.

CPSIA information can be obtained at www.ICGtesting.com
Printed in the USA
270449BV00002B/1/P

9 781414 119151